she's leaving home

she's leaving home

letting go as
my daughter goes to college

Connie Jones

Andrews McMeel
Publishing

Kansas City

This story is true. A handful of names and insignificant details have been altered for the sake of clarity and courtesy.

02 03 04 05 06 RDH 10 9 8 7 6 5 4 3 2 1

Library of Congress Cataloging-in-Publication Data

Jones, Constance M.
　She's leaving home : letting go as my daughter goes to college / Connie Jones.
　　p. cm.
　ISBN 0-7407-2346-4
　1. Jones, Constance M. 2. Mothers and daughters—
　Biography. 3. Mothers—Psychology.
　4. College students—Family relationships. 5. Separation (Psychology). 6. Life change events. I. Title.

HQ755.85 .J68 2002
306.874'3'092—dc21

2001055203

ATTENTION: SCHOOLS AND BUSINESSES

Andrews McMeel books are available at quantity discounts with bulk purchase for educational, business, or sales promotional use. For information, please write to: Special Sales Department, Andrews McMeel Publishing, 4520 Main Street, Kansas City, Missouri 64111.

Contents

Acknowledgments

My thanks to the many people—friends and relatives near and far—whose concern for Cary and our family supported us through this great rite of passage and who saw their own stories interwoven with ours. Some of you will find yourselves mentioned in these pages with gratitude. Thanks especially to Lee Ann Avery, Barbara Clancy, Paul Clancy, Sue Crommelin, Beverley Dabney, Kathryn Forrester, Ellen Sell, and Jim Sell, who read the manuscript and offered comments and encouragement. Molly Wolf has my special gratitude for giving me exactly the sort of real assistance and endorsement that I needed most. Major thanks go to my terrific agent, Linda Roghaar.

My husband, Bill, is the big hero of this enterprise; he stood by me during the birth of this book as faithfully as he did at the birth of our two children. I am grateful to David too—not only because he has been an unfailingly generous and devoted brother to Cary but also because I so admire his own bold claim to his destiny in the world as he embarks on foreign travel, college, and life away from home. I grieve and celebrate a second time around.

Of course it is to Cary above all that I owe this book, and, therefore, with much love, I dedicate it to her, as she bravely sets out in the world of adulthood with a heart full of hope.

Letter to Readers and Introduction

We loaded up the old station wagon, drove six hundred miles north from Virginia to our daughter's new college, and unloaded an astonishing collection of personal paraphernalia into a small dormitory room. After assembling lamps, arranging for a telephone hookup, and listening distractedly to some welcoming speeches, we turned around and left this beloved and cherished child to her new life apart from us. Far too soon it seemed, we turned the car back toward home, knowing with utter certainty that we were traveling in the wrong direction, because we were driving away from that which our heart loved most in the world.

If death and taxes are what we can be most sure of in this world, we can be just as sure that our children will leave home. Not everyone sends children to college, and for some families the stark, abrupt separation is blunted or attenuated by having their eighteen-year-olds commute to a local college or begin work. But more than a million and a half families in America every year see their children off to their first year in college, and it is far from easy. After all the nurturing, and sometimes the struggling, after seeing college as a bright and shining prize—when the time comes to face the separation, we react with something approximating terror.

Much has been published about getting into college, and plenty more has been written about how to succeed in college once there. But there is very little to console us parents for our grief, or to tell the story of *our* rite of passage, our letting go.

The parents I know—the ones with college-age children now and those who know their time will come—want to hear stories. They ask about that day we left our daughter, Cary, in her dorm room and drove back home. They ask how Cary's brother, David, is adjusting. They ask me over and over, as one would ask someone suffering from a grave disease, "How are you doing?"

I have written this book for them, and for you as well.

I have also, quite honestly, written it for myself. Why? As a clarification, perhaps, or a consolation. To put it plainly, to tell the stories and to name the fear and the pain and the hope is to endure, and to find rightness and even joy in it all. For me, to tell the stories is to see what it all means—not only for me, but for all of us. I hope that *She's Leaving Home* will be of value to you, not as a blueprint for the last year of high school and the one when college begins, because your own stories will be different from mine, but to let you know that somehow we are all swimming in the same river, that we are not alone, and that it is good.

she's leaving home

Chapter 1—Looking for Signs

Eternal Spirit, Earth-maker, Pain-bearer, Life-giver,
Source of all that is and shall be,
Father and Mother of us all,
Loving God, in whom is heaven,
enfold this family with your grace.
May their home be a place of your presence,
your forgiveness, and your freedom.
May your will be done in them and through them
this day and forever. Amen.[1]

Hadley in April—Sunday Night

I am sitting in a cheap motel in Hadley, Massachusetts, where, even though it's mid-April, a light snow is falling and sticking to the parked cars and in the branches of the pine trees outside the window. Cary is watching *Jaws* on TV and seems much calmer about our reason for being here than I am. Right now, Smith and Mount Holyoke are all the same to her, but by the week's end she will decide whether one of them will be her college for the next four years. They have both accepted her and have offered her nearly identical scholarships.

---

1. A prayer for the family and home, *A New Zealand Prayer Book*
   (Auckland: Collins, 1989), 759.

Cary has a checklist, and even though her list seems a bit eccentric to me, I know there is a process here that is as complicated and delicate as weather forecasting, and equally mysterious to me. She wants to know whether each dorm room is wired for computer access, how much math and science she will be expected to take, and how likely it is that she will be assigned to a private room. It's hard to imagine that the number of movies shown on campus each week serves as some manifestation from the heavens, but it's on her list, and who is to say through what channel her answer will come?

This weeklong trip in April was astronomically difficult for both of us to engineer. The number of things that had to be arranged so I could be absent from teaching all week was spectacular, the number of balls I had to drop dizzying. A week off from school was difficult for Cary too, with all her Advanced Placement exams looming.

On the road, while Cary was sleeping, a wave rolled over me, and it was the total and certain knowledge that in less than half a year I would begin to lose her. She has said, "I'm ready to get out of the South; I'm ready to go someplace entirely new," and I know that my job is to say yes. I must open the hands that want to clasp her closer to prevent the loss, and I know it. But the magnitude of what comes next takes my breath away. She will begin by being a person of this family, this home, who is "going away" to college, and she will come home eager to see her friends and to sleep late in her own bed. ("You aren't going to do anything to my room?" she has already asked.) But by the end of college, being away will be the natural thing, and our home will be a place for short visits. I know it. I have seen it happen, and I did it myself. Now it is her turn.

I love seeing her every day, and my heart is so often filled with joy just looking at her, appreciating her wit and joking with her, accommodating her vegetarianism, feeling her presence in the household, admiring her good sense and her diligence at school. How will Bill and I endure her absence? Can I talk her into a Virginia college? Shall I regret sending her to kindergarten so young, when my heart might now have had a year's reprieve?

No. My job is to help her grab this prize of freedom and new life, and to take one giant step back. This is going to be far from easy.

We must go to dinner now, even though on TV the shark is still stalking its victims, while happy children splash unaware in the surf. I take her to Mount Holyoke tomorrow for two days, to Smith on Thursday and Friday. The scholarships have to be accepted or refused by Friday afternoon.

The Brown Box

It began in tenth grade, and then by eleventh grade the college brochures began to jam the mailbox—sometimes three or more of them a day. They had pictures of smiling, healthy college students, color pictures taken mostly in the fall. Here were beautiful campuses filled with young people who appeared to be both devoted to their studies and warmed by rosy, hearty social relationships as well. There were pictures of dorm rooms—spacious, neat, and airy. Ah, advertising. Few of the colleges risked humor, but one tri-fold had the startling statement on its front in huge bold letters: "We Know Who You Are, And We Know What You've Been Doing." Inside was a suggestion that this college was seeking students with high school records like Cary's.

Apparently it was having taken the SATs that turned on this tap—no, this fire hose. Did the colleges have access to the scores? In any case, they seemed all of one mind: They wanted Cary's attention. We got a brown cardboard box for her to file the brochures in. Soon, we insisted she keep it in her room.

At first, Cary was excited and flattered by the attention from colleges, many of which she'd never heard of. She read the first few brochures. She looked up the colleges in the *Princeton Review.* She developed rules for selection that shifted from week to week, and whose seriousness Bill and I sometimes doubted. Special consideration for colleges in the *Review* that were ranked high on "dorms like palaces," and "football stadium, do we have a football stadium?" But she did not, to our surprise, eliminate women's colleges. We let her deal with her mail as she saw fit.

Before long, she was chucking the envelopes into the box unopened. Some colleges got so little attention that their mailings were never even retrieved from under piles of advertisements from the Franklin Mint and catalogs from Eddie Bauer. Multiple communications from certain colleges didn't turn her head, nor did slick and colorful viewbooks or big posters that came in long mailing tubes. Can I even estimate now how many colleges wrote her? More than a hundred. Fewer than a thousand.

By spring of her junior year, we all saw the handwriting on the wall. The good news, that so many colleges were interested in Cary, was also the bad news: *There are too many choices.*

We embarked on exploratory trips in the full and certain knowledge that a totally rational, all-inclusive search was going to be impossible. There were too many colleges, too many variables, too many uncertainties about the future. Any solution would be a proximate one. The loss of control began about now.

Cary's anxiety level about all this remained in the cool range. Ours rose, in inverse proportion to her calm.

I suspect that more than anything else, we resembled the cat on the way to the vet: we had the good sense to be apprehensive about what was coming up, but we were ridiculously uncomprehending about the nature of what we were getting ourselves into.

Dream

I am frightened by an intruder. David and I are here together; Bill is away. Terrified, I yell to him to bring me knives to defend us.

It is Cary, and she attacks me, aiming for my lower abdomen. Carefully, almost surgically, I slip the knives into the same part of her. She stops advancing and slowly lowers herself onto my body, bleeding, but apparently not mortally wounded. She softens, and our abdominal pains meld together. She will survive.

Bill, or the police, arrive. I send David off to bring a gift. He does so, and he carefully wraps it in beautiful paper and makes a card with a large C on it just as they arrive.

Waking from this dream, I discovered that I had abdominal cramps, and I shook my head in wonder for about the thousandth time at how physical experience is woven into dreams where it takes on meaning in the context of a story. Events of the day, too, because that morning, my friend Charlie and I had talked, heart touching heart, about our daughters and their growing up. That afternoon, Cary received her first college acceptance letter.

Cary has attacked my feminine place, my womb perhaps, and I hers. There is something that each of us has killed in the other, yet we both will survive. She rises up from me and is a little surly, but in a way that I instantly recognize is normal and healthy.

Throughout these events, David is calm, as if all is perfectly normal with his sister and his mother.

I wonder again about the wisdom that is contained in dreams and why it is so veiled and metaphorical. I know that this dream is about mother and daughter, and I sense that Cary and I are being granted a certain wisdom in this couple of years that we do not consciously know we have access to, to do something terribly difficult and painful and necessary. We are not oblivious or inarticulate about our parting from each other—we both have the gift of observation and awareness. This dream makes sense to me: a new and fertile young woman who has come from a womb now close to infertility is growing to womanhood. She will take up her new life, and she will depart from my old life. There is a hint of rivalry here, maybe even jealousy. Her aggressiveness and surliness, though, are a gift—to her, as a tool, to me, as a way of forcing me to keep my distance. Certainly there is pain. Yet there is also a bond between us, and an acceptance of the rightness of it all that heals the wounds. The wounds are somehow honored.

Is the fact that the men are absent or oblivious disturbing? Perhaps this just is not their job—it is our business to transact. No, there may be more to it than that—there is the beautiful gift David brings, as if to pay homage to something—Cary's emerging womanhood and fecundity? Her breaking free of the mother? Her reaching toward fullness of life?

As so many times before when marveling at a dream, I ask, where does this all come from, and to whom can I return thanks?

Taking the Tour

We are in an information session at what the college guides call a "highly competitive" private school. In a spacious, well-lighted room with movable chairs and lots of marble and glass and video equipment, a dozen or two casually but neatly dressed and attentive parents sit with their college-applicant children, also well dressed, near them. There are quite a number of younger siblings who are bored and fidgety. They are being shushed and are probably being bribed with promises of treats after the ordeal is over. Each family unit is readily identifiable, because one or two chairs are left between them and the next family.

The admissions counselors are, every last one of them, beautiful, and all of them are recent graduates of this college. The men are trim and tanned, in coat and tie. Not suits, though—khaki pants and unbuttoned blazers, and colorful ties. They wouldn't be confused with funeral directors. The women are slim and energetic, in brightly colored linen dresses. All these young people are well scrubbed and enthusiastic, and they practically sparkle. You would be proud to have your own child turn out like this, you think.

These presenters have it down to a well-tuned performance. Not too long, either: a pitch, a few jokes, a little video, Q & A, and a great deal of earnestness. They know their audience. How many audiences have they seen, just like this one?

The parents are as acutely focused on the presentation as any patient might be, listening to diagnosis and treatment options from a doctor. Focused, but maybe also a little stunned to be in this position.

If the parents are drinking in every word, the applicants themselves seem to be blinking on and off. It's hard to shoulder the responsibility of engineering your future in a consistent way when you're seventeen, without laying it down every now and then. (The children's inattention to taking charge of their future drives their parents crazy, of course, whether it's at this college visit or at home.)

The admissions counselors never flag in their patience or their ability to be personable. It's their job, and they have plenty of practice.

The parents ask the questions, not the young people.

The matter of the total cost of this college is raised, and when a figure in the neighborhood of $30,000 is spoken out loud, there is a brief moment of total and silent awe in the room. The parents do not flinch, maybe because they already know the number, or maybe because registering shock or dismay would be too embarrassing, even mortifying. They've known all these years how terribly expensive college would be, yet they are ashamed that they have not somehow managed to pull the rabbit out of the hat and amass enough money to stroke a check for this. Maybe they are still harboring a hope for a big scholarship. Maybe they have recently talked with a banker and are resigned to taking out a second mortgage. Maybe they are trying to conceal that they are hyperventilating at the thought of spending such a sum of money, or having to tell their child that they can *not* spend such a sum of money. It is a very full moment.

Some of the prospective students, though, *do* react to the figure quoted. I see one of them look with raised eyebrows and open mouth at his father, but his father, stony-faced, does not return his son's gaze. I sit there imagining dialogue between father and son and lose track of what the admissions counselor is saying. I tune back in. An answer is being given to a worried mother about campus security—after-dark call boxes and key cards that let residents into dormitories but keep potential predators out. I pay closer attention. No, the word "predators" was not used by the admissions team. My interpolation, of course.

I like this college, and I admire their extraordinarily polished presentation. There doesn't seem to be much fake razzle-dazzle, either. The counselors seem more or less to be telling the truth about the place, and I can't help liking them. This college, of course, probably has applicants out the ears and is far from needing to attract any who have a wrong impression of the place or who might turn out to be unhappy once they enroll.

I smile my approval as one parent asks, "What do students say they do *not* like about this college?" Great question. Another asks, "Is it true that you keep track of the number of times a prospective student contacts you?" Then there is a ripple of appreciative laughter from parents for another question: "Can we pay tuition on a credit card to get a *lot* of frequent-flier miles?" No, you can't. But they're working on it.

We are all assigned in groups to guides who will take us on our campus tours. These are current students, also cheerful and well scrubbed, but wearing shorts and T-shirts and sandals. We've been on these tours before. We've developed a theory of what the job qualifications must be for tour guides.

- Must be good-looking, healthy, and bright-eyed.
- Must look like somebody you would want your son or daughter to date.
- Must be able to walk backward along sidewalks without looking or stumbling.
- Must be perky but have a voice like a bullhorn.
- Must exude enthusiasm for college, good humor, and *joie de vivre*.

But I wonder as we trek along paths and up hills, peer into dormitory rooms and bathrooms, survey the lunchtime menu (are there vegetarian alternatives?), and notice classrooms with fewer than twenty desks in them (carefully chosen, no doubt, to emphasize small class size)—are these tours for the parents or the kids? And have the kids noticed anything that is going to change the shape and direction of their lives, if they are drawn to this place?

Overheard in the Grocery Store

Customer speaking to another customer, obviously a friend:

"What do you know about the job market in Atlanta?"

"I dunno. There's plenty of hospitals there. Why?"

"Because Meg is applying to Agnes Scott as well as American and William and Mary. And I'm thinking of moving to D.C. or Atlanta, you know, where she is. After the divorce, I have no reason to stay here, and with only one child . . ."

"I have no idea about jobs in Atlanta or D.C., but I have some advice."

"Really? What?

"Stay here. Or go to Alaska if you want. But let Meg go."

"Well, maybe you're right."

"I'm right."

Robert

I was talking with a student of mine named Robert recently, a young man probably in his late twenties who is both competent and ambitious. He asked me earnestly, paying great attention to what I might say, whether he should transfer from our community college next fall to the College of William and Mary, or to James Madison University. He knows that William and Mary, Thomas Jefferson's alma mater, has a national reputation, so his degree might in some manner be "worth more" as he goes on to graduate or law school. But he really doesn't like Williamsburg as much as Harrisonburg, and he has a multitude of friends at JMU. What did I think?

I told Robert that I couldn't choose his college for him but that he'd come to the right place to talk about this matter of selecting a college that had selected him. I told him about Cary.

"How about arranging to spend a couple of days, including a day going to classes, at each of the two?" I suggested. "Do everything, go everywhere, talk with everybody. Listen to professors, find some parties that will invite you in, eat their food, take a tour, get lost on the campus, question anybody who will pay attention to you. Above all, look for signs."

"What?" Robert asked. He had been with me up to that point. "Look for what?"

"I don't know what," I said. "Signs. Trust me. Something will happen that will make your decision clear. But you have to be watching carefully."

He frowned and considered. I think he understood. If he opened himself up to being guided, if he kept his eyes open, he might see, well, *something*. I didn't tell him to say his prayers first, because I didn't know Robert well enough to know whether he was a praying person.

"If you squint hard enough in the dark, sometimes there's a faint light that pulls you onto one path rather than another," I said.

My memory of my own college application process resembles a box with just a few fading leftover photographs in it. It was more than thirty years ago. But I remember that decision time well. For the first time in my life I knew that making a choice would take me decisively in one direction and not another. That choosing one path would exclude the others.

I visited Mount Holyoke College when it was sleeting. The campus was bleak and deserted that day, the sidewalks accumulating a sheet of ice, but I remember the moment at which I received the sign. A solitary student swathed in heavy winter clothes came up a sloping path as my parents and I and a campus tour guide walked down it. As the student passed, she smiled and looked straight in my eye and said (as if as a gracious host she was willing to take responsibility for the foul weather), "This place is beautiful when spring comes, really it is!"

That was all. On the basis of that greeting, I went to Mount Holyoke. It sounded flimsy then, and it still does. But it was enough.

Had I prayed for a sign? Perhaps, but I doubt it. All the same, I consider that one sentence from a stranger to have been a message from heaven. Judge as you will.

I cannot tell about Cary's prayers, or even her anxieties. I know that my advice to her, while I have meant it to be comforting and encouraging, has also been contradictory and confusing, no doubt because of the great mystery I see in all this. I have told her that there are hundreds of colleges that would receive her with open arms, and dozens that would serve her well. I have told her that her application file at the colleges to which she's applied probably has inspired racing pulses around admissions committee tables and maybe has even been drooled on. I have said that if she makes the wrong choice, it can be repaired; transferring from one college to another is commonplace and sensible these days. Much easier than getting a divorce, far less painful, and nothing even to feel guilty about.

But I have also told her to choose several colleges that seem right and apply to all of them. Complete the applications and visit the schools. Then open your heart and watch for signs. The right answer will appear.

How will she know the right answer when she sees it?

I don't know, I say, but you will know.

We'll see what happens, I say—to Cary, and to everyone who inquires about her. Am I thinking about unforeseen scholarship offers? Am I expecting divine intervention?

Well. Maybe so.

Does Cary imagine that she will be guided, or does she join most of her peers believing she is in charge of her future? Can I hope for both?

Wait and see, I say to Cary and to Robert too. It will all work out.

I believe I'm speaking to myself as well.

Hadley in April—Thursday

The moment I left her at Mount Holyoke on Monday I missed her, and I memorized the feeling, knowing it was a preview for next September. I was glad that most of her clothes and books and papers were still in the motel room, where I returned to grade exams and read. A little of her company was there.

Cary glowered at me when I left the scheduled campus tour a little early. I had a date to meet Nancy, an Internet friend and someone who I anticipate will be a trustworthy alternative mother should Cary need one so far from home, up here in Massachusetts. I think Cary is more anxious than she shows, pulling away from me to go to college nearly six hundred miles from home, yet for just a second reaching back for her mother's hand the way a toddler does.

My turmoil and ambivalence grip me. Don't go! I want to say. You can stay at home, and I'll take care of you! (I could almost do it, I think. It wouldn't be so hard just now when she is vulnerable and open. I could overwhelm her with my will. The look of an eye could bring her up short, take years of growth toward maturity away from her. Just a very slight exertion of power would shatter her resolve to fly away on her own. I might even convince her she'd decided it herself.)

God, she really does need to save herself from me.

I tell this to Nancy over coffee in Amherst. She tells me I have not lost my mind. I know a touchstone when I see one, and Nancy is a gift straight from heaven.

In the evening I go to a reception for parents, and I am immersed in a huge room full of at-sea parents. We are probably all quite good at cocktail parties and strained social occasions, but here we are as pathetically, ridiculously adrift as shy teenagers at their first dance. There is no comfort in this room of absolute strangers, and even though every one of us knows we are as lucky as lottery winners that this lovely college wants to enroll our daughters, I can feel the weight of sadness and impending loss in the room. Confused and embarrassed at our inability to lighten the occasion or make any genuine contact with one another, we depart too quickly to our motels, to wait for the real drama to reach its climax. We've been excused from the scene our daughters are starring in, and our sips of wine from plastic cups and snacks of vegetables with dip have not distracted us from the real heart of the matter. We are like worried relatives in a waiting room, impatient for a word about the outcome of the surgery.

Back on Route 47 on the way to the motel in the woods, I turn off the radio and pray out loud that Cary will be drawn along the right path and that I will keep my hands to myself and resist the urge to interfere.

I scold myself for being close to tears as I let myself into the empty room, bathe, and go to bed.

Twice Born

I am talking with my friend Sandy.

"Do you remember those last few days before going into labor?" she says. "Your abdomen is huge and tight, like an enormous packed orange? There's this creature inside that likes to elbow and pummel you at night, that presses on your bladder so that you have to go when there's even a teaspoon of pee inside you? And you pant like an old woman when you go up the stairs? That's all if your pregnancy is going well.

"You read all the books, and you know that one of the great remaining medical mysteries is why labor starts. Sure, they can induce labor, and they can schedule you for a Caesarean, but natural labor? Who knows why it begins when it does?

"I figure, the baby just knows when it's time. It just can't stand it in there any longer; it's just time to go. And the going has got to be scarier than the first day of school, giving a speech, and walking into a dark room where the furniture's been moved, all put together. It's a drive into the unknown. I imagine that the urge to remain where it's comfortable and warm and predictable must surely occasion some little-baby sort of regret. But it is literally impossible to honor. The drive is on, the push to go. And out they come, frontward, backward, or sideward so they have to be lifted out by surgeons, but the time has come.

"And for us? The pain, the mess, the breathlessness of it, and no matter how well things are going, just a shade of panic too. Even the natural-childbirth folks among us have got to concede: a sliver of us at least would like to have been put to sleep during the whole thing. Wake me when it's over. Why do I have to do this today?

"Especially if it's our second, we know what we have in front of us. The demands, the fatigue, the disruption of a former life, never to be recovered. Here it comes again. Why was it that I thought having another child was a good idea?

"But when that urge to push comes, there is nothing in this world like it, remember? It hurts as if pain itself has come to fill the whole screen of your consciousness, as if there is nothing else in the whole world but pushing against that pain, expelling that baby. It is agony and terrific at the same time, and it is the only thing you want or need to achieve in the whole world. You take some breaths, and then the urge, the demand, to push comes again. Where does it come from? We didn't make it up, and it certainly didn't come from memorizing Lamaze manuals. It just is.

"Then the baby is born. It all makes sense now. Well, more or less. And truth be told, if that baby had waited one day longer, we'd have gone crazy, right?

"I figure that sending your children to college is sort of like this. There's something in them that wants to stay, that's afraid to leave into that big wide world. There's something in us too that wants to hold them back in the womb of our hearts and our households. But by God, there's a force stronger than both parent and child that says it's time to go. No matter how frightened they are to lurch toward independence, no matter how ill equipped for adulthood or clueless they are, they just have to do it. They'll get argumentative and nearly obnoxious sometimes, and they'll cause you pain—your love for them *is* pain in a way, like a tearing of your innermost tissues, pulling part of you away with them.

"But the time comes, and the need to push feels like all the laws of nature converging on one moment. It breaks our hearts, but we must save our own lives too. We must reclaim bodies that are not filled to bursting with this child reaching out to the world. We must yield to something so filled with wisdom that pain really does become joy, that nurturing is transformed into the independence of a new creature, and apparent hurt becomes all that is right in the universe.

"Well," Sandy says, "sometimes I think I have given birth to each of my children twice. You'll see what I mean."

Morning Prayer

Friday morning I rise early at the motel in the woods. Cary is at Smith now, and she will be occupied for hours with the student who hosted her overnight, and with activities designed to persuade her to choose Smith. Yesterday I noticed that the church on Northampton's main street, St. John's, offers Morning Prayer at seven o'clock on weekday mornings. I arrive a few minutes early.

It seems that I am the entire congregation, and the priest invites me to sit in the choir with him. We read the service from *The Book of Common Prayer,* and he reads the lessons from a version of the New Testament so contemporary in its language it makes me smile—Peterson's *The Message.*

The priest is a stranger, but I am very comfortable with him— for if two people are in a quiet church speaking to God together, how can they remain strangers for long? I ask his prayers for

Cary's discernment of the right path, and for my diocese's upcoming election of a new bishop, and he asks mine for concerns of his congregation. He gives me his blessing. I am certain that Morning Prayer this morning is a link in a chain of holy events. It's just that I can't see the pattern yet.

If Cary decides on Smith, I would not place a large wager on her ever setting foot in this church or meeting this kind man. But in a way that I can't quite explain, to have prayed with him at seven on a Friday morning seems to me to bind us all together into a connected whole, putting us in the care of a trustworthy God who directs our paths even when we least suspect it, and bids us to let go of our control over things and let benevolence be.

Heavenly Father, we say near the end of Morning Prayer, *in you we live and move and have our being: We humbly pray you so to guide and govern us by your Holy Spirit, that in all the cares and occupations of our life we may not forget you, but may remember that we are ever walking in your sight.*

A Sign

Seldom during the application process did Cary ask anything from me but my signature on the checks for the application fees. But we did talk about the practice application essays her English teacher assigned on several occasions. Cary entertained me by describing her classmates' approaches to the task. One friend wrote sparkling and bold prose that confessed his infatuation with Madonna and Cher and the popular music of the seventies.

This is the time in my life to invent a new me, Cary says. I can portray myself in these essays any way that I like. I will choose who I am.

True, I say. And it will be the time in your life when you are no longer primarily Bill and Connie's daughter, or David's sister. You will first and foremost be you yourself.

On the other hand, those essays must be faithful to some truth that you know of yourself, contain some honest bit of self-revelation. It's not just that they will be phony otherwise, and probably transparently so. It's also that however crazy and high pressure this process may seem, misrepresenting yourself to dazzle an admissions committee is a grave mistake. A college that invites a made-up Cary Jones to attend instead of the real one will probably be a terrible place for you to spend four years.

She went off and wrote her essays as she saw fit. They were honest. Some of them were funny. One had illustrations. Several colleges seemed to like the real Cary Jones enough to admit her. But now was the time to choose.

Sunday night, before I delivered her to Mount Holyoke for two days, we turned off the lights to go to sleep. I wished that we still said prayers together, as we had when she was little. I said to her in the dark, "I think I will pray now that you will be guided to make the right decision this week, and that you will see a sign pointing to the right choice. Maybe just a very little sign, but a sufficient one." I silently added, and let me be content if she sees the sign and I don't.

It came.

The visit at Mount Holyoke on Monday and Tuesday was beautifully arranged, and it was a strange thing for me to see my own alma mater wrapped up in a fancy package to encourage accepted students to enroll. How odd it was to see my old dormitories and classroom buildings, but odder still to think that Cary might, by her own choice, come here and get to know them as well as I had. But it had to be her decision. I did no lobbying.

The visit disappointed her, I could tell, but she couldn't say why. "I could come to college here. It would be all right," she said.

Wednesday we went to Boston, to the science museum and Filene's Basement, and that night we returned to the motel under the tall pines.

On Thursday she saw the sign. I will never know what she saw, or from what deep place inside her she detected it. But the message was so plain and so clear that the light of it seemed to radiate from her face. She knew.

We bought a foot-long Smith decal and plastered it onto the back car window, so that all the way home to Virginia we proclaimed the good news. The decision was made.

I did remember to say thank you for the sign.

Chapter 2—Cutting the Cord

O God, our times are in your hand:
Look with favor, we pray,
on your servant Cary as she begins another year.
Grant that she may grow in wisdom and grace,
and strengthen her trust in your goodness all the days of her life;
through Jesus Christ our Lord. Amen.[1]

Airport

There was a moment at the airport tonight, when she walked down the ramp and out of sight into the plane, that she turned and gave me a tentative wave, and then she was off, giving no more glances backward, walking with that steady head-high gait I recognize well, off for three weeks in Germany and Italy with Christina (her plane ticket her high school graduation present). I saw bravery overcome her ambivalence, and I was proud of her.

She was wearing so much metal that she set the detectors off: heavy belt buckle to hold up the long pants she prefers to shorts or skirts, steel-toed boots, and the chrome choker necklace she alternates with rhinestones these days. All day in the car we kept good company. We decided not to blame each other for being a little late and risking missing the plane. She tolerated National Public Radio

---

1. *The Book of Common Prayer* (The Episcopal Church, 1979), 830.

and my repeated advice on looking after herself on this trip. We had no arguments, as we seldom have in these nearly eighteen years. She has been what I have sometimes heard called an "easy child," easy to love and affectionate in return.

But recently there has been a metallic hardness creeping in, no doubt the need in her growing to sharpen the knife with which to cut the cord to me. She will not permit herself to be cuddled at all. She will jump just as high as her cat Sadie does when petted on the head or back. As late as a year ago (or is my memory of time failing?) she would suffer me to wake her in the morning by rubbing her back and shoulders and neck, and telling her the strangest or most scandalous stories from the newspaper I had been reading since I'd been up. Now she wakes at my word, or with the alarm, and dismisses me from behind a closed door.

At the airport she clearly wanted me to come with her to the gate, yet if she had any nervousness about the unknown several hours ahead of her (not to mention the unknown life ahead of her), she concealed it from me. (Does she acknowledge it herself?) But: Come with me to the gate. Yes, buy me my supper, please, but just give me that ten-dollar bill and I'll order my vegetable pita and deal with the vendor myself.

As we sat fairly companionably waiting for her to board, I was once again saying have fun, be safe, call me when you arrive, buy David a present, be polite to your host families.

"I hate to give you up for these three weeks," I said, "when you have so few weeks left at home." And then I added, seeing clearly, "But I guess I'd better get used to it."

She chuckled and gave me a sidelong glance. I thought for just a second I saw the knife. I said nothing. She has to cut, I know, and the wounds, whether we choose to acknowledge it or not, are to both of us, and are necessary. Otherwise, we both will perish.

I watched her march confidently down the runway to the plane, turning and waving with dismissive impatience mixed with a *soupçon* of the affection of old, holding her head high and not turning back. From my inmost breath came the whisper of a blessing, *the Lord make his face gracious to you, the Lord surround you and keep you from harm, from this day forward and for evermore.*

No Thank You

There is a woman I worked with once in Memphis whose daughter Kelly went to Smith a decade ago. I have never met Kelly, and I know nothing of her personality, her intellect, or so much as the color of her hair. But her mother, Annie, has been quite intent these last few months on putting Kelly in touch with Cary.

"I know that Cary is *seriously* considering Smith," Annie says, "and I just want Kelly to have a chance to tell her what the place is *really like* before she commits herself!" This is a woman who speaks in italics.

Kelly hated Smith within weeks of arriving there, her mother tells me, and she left by the end of her first year. Among other things, Kelly lamented, Smith students were horrid to Southerners, and she found herself with no friends.

Bill and I have talked about this.

Could it possibly be true that Tennesseans or Virginians are bound to be unhappy at all New England colleges, or perhaps at Smith in particular? Could a person like Cary who has made friends in Japan, Sicily, and the Norfolk Public Schools fail to find friends in Massachusetts? I doubt it. On the other hand, do I have a right to insulate Cary from Kelly's testimony?

There are some objective realities about colleges, I suppose, and only a fool would ignore them. If you want to play football and they have no football team, College A is wrong for you; if you want to major in Chinese and they don't teach it, College B is a poor choice. But I suspect that there are truths more powerful still: you will make of that institution something of what you envision it to be; you will have the experience that your heart fashions out of the reality that confronts you. I see this hold for the students I encounter, who show up at the doorstep of the community college where I teach. In fact, I think this holds for life in general.

Cary's heart had been won by Smith before I heard from Annie. The choice is made. Six other colleges who invited her to enroll have been forgotten. Should I let Kelly call Cary at this point?

Um. No.

My friend Nancy asks me, why do you suppose Kelly's mother is prevailing on you?

Now there's a good question. Has she a genuine desire to save a friend's daughter from a terrible fate? Or is there a festering, unresolved resentment here, a blame so much easier to lay at the doorstep of a college than to untangle painstakingly to reveal a deep truth? Is this urgent offer less to save Cary from a miserable experience and more to prevent mother and daughter's own discomfort lest Cary *not* be miserable?

I think these days selecting a college is like a knight's sacred quest, or a Native American's vision quest. As knights set off to seek the Holy Grail, or young Indians make a solitary retreat to wait upon a sign so subtle it might be the song of a nightingale, so, too, anxious high school seniors pursue something nearly as elusive, the Right College. My good sense says there are dozens, even hundreds of colleges that would serve Cary well, yet there is a single path that she and each of her friends tread alone. They have maps, but they can find their way only on their own, and the markers they see along the way may very well make sense to themselves alone. If we are careful and wise, we parents learn to stand in the shadows while the light shines on the path, and honor the sacredness and delicacy of the quest. The proper demeanor if you are witnessing a high-wire act is to hold your breath. If you interfere with the seniors' search for the right path to college, you run the risk of distracting them from an important balancing act, of blinding them at the very split second when the illumination is scheduled to come.

We parents gather at odd times—while waiting for parent-teacher conferences, at coffee hour after church, in the grocery line—and we ask about one another's children's college choices with deference and tact. We shake our heads sometimes, marveling at the surprises that surface, but not for a second ridiculing the seriousness of this choice, or the importance of our children's following their signs, however invisible they are to us. Because to so much as raise an eyebrow, I think, might upset a balance so fine that a light breeze would disturb it, might wreck a placement so right and so good that the future of the race might hinge on it, and the hand of God might be behind the whole thing.

I cannot interfere, and I cannot permit Annie and Kelly to, either. We said no thank you and wished both mother and daughter well.

Little Bird

A little Carolina wren found its way into our screened porch, and it was trapped. The cat was more than interested; she was delighted. There is no door to this porch except to inside the house, and the entry hole in the screen was too small to be useful now. The bird was frantic.

Cary and I banished the cat, and we tried to capture the bird with a sheet. No go. BANG went the bird into the front screen. BANG into the back screen. Little bird, we said, we are trying to help you. BANG. We ran to borrow crab net from a neighbor. (Since we live near the water, nearly everyone has one.) We cornered the bird and I slipped the net over her. She instantly escaped through the holes. I tried and failed again. A brainstorm: panty hose! Cary and I stretched panty hose on the nether side of the net, so that the bird would escape into a soft mesh.

It didn't work. The poor bird flew back and forth, smashing into screens, sitting loftily atop the ceiling fan that was not on, briefly resting. Cary and I were getting as frustrated as the bird. We cursed the Ping-Pong table that got in our way. We even had a brief go at blaming each other. We had a net, some panty hose, and a sheet, but these and goodwill were not enough.

Come here, little bird, I said. We are your friends. We are your mommies. We would like to take you outside where the cool wind and the rain and the leaves are. Please cooperate. We talked to the bird as if we could gentle it with the tone of our voices. No. We resorted to smashing the net around again.

I invoked the name of St. Francis, because I happened to know that it was one day on the church calendar from the celebration of his feast day. Could he really talk to animals? He might have talked some sense into this panicky bird, calmed it with his spirit.

We aren't St. Francis, you know, little bird. But we are trying our best to let you go back outdoors where you belong. Let us catch you gently so we can set you free.

This time when I pinned the bird against the screen with the net that had a complete pair of panty hose dangling from it, Cary slipped a sheet behind. For a terrible second I thought we had killed it, or that it had died of fright, because it was still as we carried it outside. But the minute we released it, it flew exuberantly away.

Now here is the strangest part of the story of all. That Carolina wren flew to the big muscular arm of a great elm tree in our front yard. It sat there where I could see it. Have a nice bird life, I said, and turned away. But it didn't move. I went to set dishes in the sink and came back. It was still sitting exactly in the same place as if it had been sculpted there. I answered a phone call and returned. It was still there. For fully forty-five minutes, this plain but beautiful little brown bird with the stripe through its eye remained in our precincts. Tired perhaps, or maybe acknowledging that this place was important in its life, and from a point of safety was taking stock of it. Another half hour later, it was gone. Cary and I went back to our very ordinary tasks.

The bird, the children, what we create—they pass through our hands and our care, our earnest and fumbling and strenuous care. They pause for just a moment to consider where they have been, and then they are off, in another's hands and care. We go to great lengths to set them free, but we have these moments of great regret and sadness when they go.

Late Nights in the Summer

I woke up at three in the morning to hear the shower running. Cary had been home since midnight after an evening with her friends at a movie and then the Open House diner, which like its name says, never closes. Most nights since returning from Italy she has gone out with her friends. Then she will urge us to go to bed while she stays up, doing laundry, reading or watching a movie on television, and checking her huge volumes of e-mail. One night I got up and complained about the late hour and the water running so long, the noise in the bathroom. Since then she has showered downstairs.

Out of consideration? Certainly. But also to protect her privacy and to enjoy her solitude on her own terms, not the household's.

It's not that she can really sleep late most mornings—she has a job as a counselor and lab assistant at a summer science camp for kids—but she naps in the afternoons. These sleeping patterns may be practice for college, but they are also her way of still being *in* the household, while less and less *of* it. Now it seems that she is physically and emotionally just passing through. She is sorting her possessions in her room.

We excused her from church this morning, because she is tired and because she doesn't want to go—arguments that would probably have been overridden until now. She has made atheistic pronouncements for months, has sometimes been rude, as if seeking either to offend or to provoke a response. It occurs to me that she needs to cut the cord to God just now, as well as the one to her parents. Her attendance at church lately reminds me of the patience of a captive just before freedom, of a slave who takes one more beating in silence the evening before an escape on the Underground Railroad. I am offended, I'm afraid, just as she intends, but I know that it is her soul now, her choice and responsibility to handle God without me. In the early hours of the morning I woke with a prayer in my mind that was half from me, half to me, commending Cary to God's care, whether she knows she is being cared for or not.

My job as a mother is not yet done. In these last weeks there is so much to be planned and bought and packed. There is nurturing yet to do. But I feel the many threads that have bound her to me for eighteen years being released, one by one, as if that thick and strong umbilical cord that gave her life has grown as thin as gossamer, until it can no longer be detected.

Or it is like a hot-air balloon that is throwing off the ballast that has held it down, and the lines tying it to the ground are being unhitched. The big, beautiful, colorful, lighter-than-air living thing is pulling, pulling away from the gravity of our household, bound for the skies, joyfully looking skyward and not down at the ground from which it sprang. And that's its nature, its destiny, its joy. To hold it down onto the ground would be a travesty, even a sin.

But down here on the ground, it is hard not to cry as we wave at that unspeakably beautiful thing, seeing it drift soundlessly away in its own breathless journey, becoming smaller and smaller against the cloudless blue sky.

Almost Fall

I went for a bike ride after dinner—part of another new exercise regime. I suppose I had the idea because earlier in the day I'd asked Cary whether she wanted to take her old beach cruiser to college. She hadn't answered. Some things she will make decisions about, others not. Just ten days from leaving, she has yet to shift into high gear. I'm having trouble with this myself.

Cary was out with her friends. Only the ones going to the University of Virginia remain. All summer the cast of friends has shifted, depending on who is available because of jobs and travel, but now the stage is getting bare. Still, she wants to be with friends at night, or with David, or by herself. Already I am seeing much less of her, and she will not allow herself to be touched.

Was now a good time to flip these handlebars back to their normal position? Cary changed them to point downward when she got the bike years ago, when she was smaller, but they are quite a reach for me. She has used this bicycle very seldom, and I will probably inherit it in a week or so. I could ask Bill to get the wrench out tonight. No—that would be a mistake. People have said that in the first year they are away at college, you shouldn't change their rooms beyond making the bed with clean sheets. While they eagerly leap into that unknown world that is beckoning them, they want to keep open the option of sliding back into the known and familiar at a moment's notice. And by God, it must be exactly familiar. The handlebars will get changed eventually, but not right now.

As I pedaled easily around this comfortable residential neighborhood while dusk descended, I felt a faint breeze of cooler air— definitely a promise of fall. Yes, the wheels crackled through some early dry leaves. And all of a sudden I was visited by a vivid image of Halloween.

Cary hasn't trick-or-treated for years, but she loves it so much that she wrote a Halloween essay on one of her college applications. It has been my favorite holiday with the children too, and it always fell to me to escort them as they trick-or-treated, shuffling door-to-door through leaves like these. The light always looked just the way it did now; the air smelled just like this.

And it will never be the same again. Even David is too old now. Still riding the bike in the dim light, I literally cried out in pain. I am losing it all! I haven't enjoyed these seventeen years enough, and I can't remember it all. I never took pictures of all her Halloween costumes; I made too little celebration of her sixteenth birthday. I can't replay those events again, can't have her girlhood back, can't hold on to her.

"Ah, Jesus!" I cried aloud into the now-dark street, but I was out of words and didn't know what to ask. It was the kind of cry you utter if you suffer a swift and unexpected ripping pain in the very center of you.

She was still out when I returned, so I couldn't run to embrace her after I put the bike in the garage. She wouldn't have permitted me to hold her in any case.

I remember what she wrote in that essay. She had the biggest dress-up collection in the neighborhood, and in the days before Halloween kids came to our house to borrow items for their costumes. The red straw hat was popular, or the black academic gown, or the silver-glitter high heels. Children would come to borrow this or that and stay for hours playing make-believe. In these later years Cary has collected thrift-store purchases—odd bits of clothing that she wears in novel combinations, trying on different looks, different selves, having the freedom to hide behind shifting masks of her own choosing.

She has the newest re-creation of herself just before her.

I have already bought the plane ticket that will bring Cary home for October break, but it is Columbus Day weekend, October 12th. She will miss Halloween at home for the first time.

And the days are getting shorter.

College Entrance Essay
by Cary Jones

My pulse starts racing as the leaves drop from the multi-colored trees and my parents begin to whine about having to turn on the furnace—for I know that these are the seasonal signs of the best holiday of the whole year. When the countless cartoon specials come on television on Sunday nights and grocery lists include mass amounts of individually wrapped Milky Ways and Sweetarts, I can smell the Halloween atmosphere in the air. What better holiday is there? A chance to show off, be someone you're not, and stuff yourself silly with empty calories. A kid's fantasy.

And indeed it was my ideal fantasy as a child. I was a very shy girl, and my way of expressing myself was by changing my appearance. Since I could walk, my persona included an amazing predilection for dressing up in costumes. In fact by age six I was known as the kid with the best dress-up collection on my block—even adults came to me for Halloween costumes—and this was not a responsibility I took lightly. Halloween was the center of the year for me, and I took great pains to insure that my *Catwoman costume was the most authentic in the neighborhood and* my *vampire had the best fangs money could buy. With the help of a few hats or scarves, it was possible for me to be anything I wanted, and I wanted to be everything. For one day of the year, it was socially acceptable to masquerade as another person, and I looked forward to the opportunity to strut my stuff on the sidewalks of my neighborhood while trick-or-treating.*

As I grew older my love of costuming expanded to include my everyday wardrobe. Since I couldn't legally trick-or-treat anymore, there was a part of my subconscious that needed to receive attention from others. I filled that gap when I got to high school by making sure that the glances I got while walking down the hallway boosted my self confidence. As a way to shield my inner self from the criticism of others, I love to dress up in outlandish clothes that I find in thrift stores and yard sales. My mood and interests change so rapidly that I change my impression on others like I change my clothes. I have never quite given up the idea I clung to in my childhood—that I can be a movie star or a famous archaeologist by the hand of fate, or with the change of a costume.

Now, as I stand at the threshold of the rest of my life, I realize that I will now have to become my own person and shed my colorful skin like a butterfly breaking out of its layers of cocoon. Having spent the first seventeen years of my life building myself through trial and error, I am more prepared than most to undertake a world full of choices. Who knows, I could become a movie star or an award-winning artist—I need only to try on that costume and walk in those shoes. Out of my childhood, I will miss most of all the world of options that were presented to me on a silver platter. Yet I also realize that I need only to look in the right places to find the inspiration to become my own person. Masquerading as another person on Halloween taught me how to shield myself from the world while still maintaining the ability to explore my life's options. When I leave home to become an adult, I'll be leaving behind the happiness and worry-free lifestyle of childhood, but I'll gain new ways with which to explore the world. I have discovered, through my childhood passion for change, that the path to self-knowledge is paved with a thousand attempts to find truth.

The Binding of Isaac

Two teachers of an adult Bible class were talking about the Genesis story of Abraham and the sacrifice of Isaac. One told us about the kinds of sacrifices that Jews offered in Abraham's time and about why each detail of the story was historically significant. Both teachers were men, and both parents—one of grown children, one of toddlers. Neither of them at this moment seemed agitated by the story, but I found it harder and harder to sit still and consider what a supposedly benevolent God was asking his beloved, his chosen one, to do. Ask me to cut off my own arm, I thought, and for the sake of God, and I might be able to do it. Go into the jaws of death at the command of the Holy One? At least in my imagination, I could muster the faith to do that too.

But take my own child's life? Be asked to act so irrationally, so in contradiction to what I know of God, so in violation of love itself? Do it simply because I was commanded to do it, as a cruel test, without knowing about the ram that would appear at the last minute? This is something that cannot even be thought.

The teachers seemed to be droning, but I was not listening to them talk about the pyre and the offering of a lamb. I saw the rest of the class, mostly parents too, nodding without distress, perhaps too familiar with the story, or too confident of how it would end. Or maybe it was just that they were in a sounder frame of mind than I was.

But as for me, today, the story was simply terrifying.

One man, a father, took Abraham's plight as an artifact of a primitive and bygone era. "God clearly would not ask that of us today," he said comfortably.

"I think I disagree," I broke in, leaning forward from a back row and raising a hand and waving it a bit. "God *does* ask this of us."

"What do you mean?" one of the teachers asked.

"God is asking this of me. Right now," I said. "God is asking me to give up to an uncertain fate my oldest child. He is asking me to give up Cary to him, in fact. Because from now on, God and Cary have business together, and I have to trust God so much that I will surrender her into his care. And I am horrified."

There was a bit of silence, and then sympathetic murmuring, before we moved on. I sat back in my seat. At first blush I imagined that these Bible class companions were both embarrassed and respectful, recognizing my little speech as a naked cry from the heart, but that they had not understood me at all. On second thought, however, I knew that along with me, many of them have stood side by side with Abraham at the altar, knife in hand—have stood with me on the edge of the place for losing children, knowing that the call is to act and not shrink back, that the choice is not ours. Maybe on this particular Sunday morning I had exposed the terrible truth again, and they had remembered. There was a moment of quiet, one of those fractions of a second when all is clear and truthful and sharp, before time and ordinariness resume.

Then I wept in church. Fortunately, this is the sort of place where if you do that, someone will hold you and bless you. But how indeed can you trust such a terrible God whose love is so radical and so sufficient in the face of all this terror, a God who sacrificed a son? And how without that trust could I even get out of bed in the morning?

Then Abraham put forth his hand, and took the knife to slay his son. But the angel of the Lord called to him from heaven, and said, "Abraham, Abraham!" And he said, "Here I am." He said, "Do not lay your hand on the lad or do anything to him; for now I know that you fear God, seeing you have not withheld your son, your only son, from me." . . . "Because you have done this, and have not withheld your son, your only son, I will indeed bless you, and I will multiply your descendants as the stars of heaven and as the sand which is on the seashore." [2]

Oh, God, I see what I am being asked to do.

---

2. Genesis 22:10–12, 16–17 *(New Revised Standard Version).*

Red Flower

I was in San Antonio, Texas, grading Advanced Placement U.S. History essays with five hundred other historians who probably, like me, were making extra money to pay college tuition for their children. Grimly repetitive work, mind-numbing. Trapped there for a week in the summer, I painfully knew that the time was drawing very near to say good-bye to Cary. Although I knew how little time and attention she invested in the household these days, I felt like a misplaced person, and my heart regretted I was a thousand miles away instead of at home, keeping watch.

Hour after hour, we read exams, hundreds of them, over a thousand by week's end. Steamy though Texas is in the summer, this third-floor grading room was overly air-conditioned, and I'd brought a favorite red sweatshirt and even socks to my grading place. Sometimes I'd read standing up, to stay awake and alert, and sometimes I'd sit on the floor. Each of these essays was written by someone's beloved child, after all. I needed to pay attention. Occasionally I'd take a dozen exams outside, to grade on the sun-baked balcony.

I stepped outdoors one weary afternoon, at tree-top level, to read yet another explanation of the origin of political parties. Still and quiet, I read for quite some time and then looked up. Zooming in at less than an arm's length was a huge, now hovering dragonfly. No! It was a hummingbird! In the two blinks of an eye it took me to realize why it was there, the bird saw with disappointment that I was not, in fact, the biggest red flower in the universe.

I spoke to the bird and said, "Good luck, dear thing—a good life and many flowers to you." And my heart lifted with the certainty that I could offer the very same blessing to my daughter as I let her go.

Poem

A poem from Cary, age five, to her mother:

> *I love you*
> *Violets are*
> *blue*
> *Dark is lightless*
> *but you*
> *are priceless.*

Chapter 3—The Day Comes

Almighty God, we entrust all who are dear to us
to your never-failing care and love,
for this life and the life to come,
knowing that you are doing for them better things
than we can desire or pray for;
through Jesus Christ our Lord. Amen.[1]

Self-portrait

Cary sketched a self-portrait in pastels when she was fourteen, and it hangs beside the staircase where I see it every day as I walk upstairs. If you were to draw a diagonal line from upper left to lower right, it would intersect the point between the open, calm, and inquiring blue-green eyes. In the upper right half of the picture you see one eye partly hooded by tawny red hair falling in a graceful wave, with a contrasting background of green so green it is the color of new life. In the lower left half of the portrait, Cary's face and jawline fade imperceptibly into white, a kind of unknown from which she has come, not holding her in place, not too precisely defining her.

---

1. *The Book of Common Prayer*, 831.

It is a lovely and serious face you see here, a young face that does not yet know all that the world has in store; anchored only with the lightest ties to past and future. The eyes look forthrightly and honestly into the here and now of all life has to offer.

It is a portrait of youth itself, I think, and I see innocence and openness. My heart yearns to protect it from all harm, perhaps even from the life of the world that the eyes are so coolly seeking. But that is not to be.

The Last Night

She is out with friends, as usual, and I have just come home from work after ten. We will be leaving tomorrow. There is a mound of stuff in the living room, waiting to be piled into the car. Piles of stuff don't shock me; this house wouldn't get a neatness award.

But it is when I go into the upstairs bathroom that I truly notice that she will be gone. The facial-care products and other chemical things that have inhabited the top drawer of the vanity and have spilled out onto its surfaces most of the time are gone, except for the rejects. There's my comb, and a couple of mismatched earrings, with some nearly gone dental floss containers. There are only two rhinestone necklaces still hanging on the towel rack over the vanity, where yesterday there were more than a dozen. A strange place to keep necklaces, you might say, but for some reason she housed her thrift-store collection of rhinestone necklaces in the bathroom, and now that it is gone I realize that it was more beautiful and dazzling and festive than I can possibly describe. To see that towel rack empty is tantamount to seeing the entire house void of its people and its contents.

Cary is still out and it's after midnight. As the summer has matured, she has been up later and later and has found her own ways to marshal and shape herself for her new life. Her staying-up stamina outlasts David's, though he sometimes watches movies with her. He's holding on to her a little, maybe memorizing her companionship, his trust for her. What is it that she is tasting and holding on to?

I'd really rather not cry as I did in church on Sunday. I'm a thinking and doing kind of person, not a weeping one. But there are times when even the most rational and stony of us give way.

I am not afraid for Cary's future, and I have no reservations about Smith. Her life is not mine to manage. I remember that Anne Lamott in one of her books quotes a friend of hers, who says in exasperation to a controlling mother something like, "Mom, if I had two lives, I'd give you one, but I don't!" Cary's life belongs to her, and she is growing in her knowledge of that, and her sense of power. Cary's life also belongs to God.

I confess that my imagination does conjure up car wrecks and predatory men, negligent professors and self-inflicted nutritional deficiencies. I can frighten myself into fear for the separation. But the truth of the matter is terribly simple. I am going to miss having Cary nearby at least a little bit every day. I'm going to miss the sound and the clutter and the smell of her nearby, the pleasure of looking at her lovely softness and her rhinestones, the enjoyment of her wit and intelligence in the house. She is my beloved first-born, the joy of my heart. How can it possibly be right that I have to give her up? My intellect knows of the rightness, but my heart grieves.

And I go to bed, to sleep, breathing a prayer for her, but also for me, for my bereavement.

Changing Tires

There is also this to consider.

One day last year Cary and I visited Hollins College for an interview. It was over Christmas vacation, and the day was very, very cold. As we drove over Afton Mountain on I-64 toward Staunton in the predawn darkness, we could barely detect broad patches of black ice peeking out from under the snow that was blowing across the interstate. Once the day dawned, we began to see car after car in the ditch beside the road. But ever mindful of our appointment, filled with the importance of our mission, we soldiered on and arrived in Roanoke to a dazzlingly beautiful day, piles of snow underfoot and clear blue sky above. We toured, we listened and poked our noses into dorm rooms, we trekked about crunching snow on the paths, and we asked questions.

By early afternoon, when we were ready for the long haul back to Norfolk, the temperature still had not risen above freezing.

Those patches of ice might be waiting to bedevil our return trip. But no, it was smooth sailing for mile after countless afternoon mile of snowy middle-of-nowhere scenery so bright that sunglasses were in order.

Then *POW*! Driving and holding the wheel, I instantly knew what had happened. We had blown a tire, the right front one. The car, bless its intrepid Swedish heart, steered straight and true, and I pulled to the side of the road.

I couldn't even remember when I'd last seen an exit. There was nothing in sight but road, cars rushing past, and an endless vista of snowbanks. After inspecting the damage, which I'd certainly diagnosed correctly, I fished out my AAA card to find the toll-free number for roadside assistance. Months ago, I'd questioned Bill's wisdom in insisting that I have a car phone, but I've been rescued by it enough times by now to be a believer. AAA would have a wrecker to us, they said, in half an hour. Or so.

We waited. And then we waited a bit more, talking at first, but both of us growing impatient. Finally, Cary said, "Where's the instruction manual for this car?" I pulled it out of the glove compartment for her.

"I'm going to change this tire," she said. "Where's the spare? Where's the jack?"

Well, I didn't know. I'd never changed a tire. "Have *you* changed a tire?" I asked.

"Not until now," she said. "But I have a good party tonight, and I don't want to miss it."

Well *all-righty* then.

We found the tire, the jack, and the tools. Reading directly out of the manual, Cary assembled the jack and removed the hubcap. The lug nuts proved to be a bit of a problem, since her heft was insufficient to budge them. I lent my superior *avoirdupois* to the task, standing on the tool to loosen each one. She put the jack where it was supposed to go and hoisted up the car. She was definitely pleased with her own progress so far. She removed the old exploded tire, replaced it with the spare, screwed the lug nuts back on, lowered the car, and together we did our best to tighten the bolts. Cary replaced the hubcap, threw everything into the back of the car, and off we went. We called AAA to tell them that since they'd been so busy pulling other peoples' cars out of snowbanks, we'd changed the tire ourselves.

As he headed back to Norfolk my heart lifted an inch or so. If she can read a manual and change a tire, I believe she'll do well on her own. Far better, I suspect, than I will do without her. A good lesson for a college visit.

And she got to the party on time.

But wait. There is an epilogue.

A couple of exits down the highway I began to worry about the air pressure in this never-used, decade-old spare, so we left the road to find a gas station. Although these days you are far more likely to find snack food and fireworks at a gas station than you are someone who can check your air for you, I thought we should stop.

We pulled up to the pumps, and I made my decision. Not sure

how Cary the tire-changer of the self-reliant generation would judge my strategy, I approached a middle-aged man pumping gas into his pickup truck.

"Excuse me," I said. "My daughter's just changed the tire on this station wagon, and we need to check the air pressure in the spare. I wonder if you could show us how?"

"Sure," he said. "Let me check it for you. Pull your car over here."

The air pressure was fine. "But you have a problem here," he said. "You've put the lug nuts on inside-out. The beveled side goes this way. Here. I've got tools. Won't take a minute."

And it didn't take much more than a minute for him to reverse the nuts and tighten them up.

"Good thing you checked," he said. "I'll bet that if you kept going down the road like that, they'd have unscrewed themselves and the tire'd have flown right off that car at sixty miles an hour."

Good thing indeed.

As we pulled back onto the interstate and continued on to Norfolk, I thought that each of the three of us might interpret this episode differently. Was it about kindness and saving lives? A *mishna,* a good deed? What about trusting in the benevolence of good people whom Providence deigns to put in our paths? About the value of a good tool kit and an auto-mechanics course? Or was it simply about the role of chance in the events that govern our lives?

Cary will keep this story as her own and decide.

I remembered to say thank you to our deliverer, and to Providence as well.

And Bill and I made sure to buy her a well-stocked tool chest to take to college.

Broken Mirror

Among the pile of things waiting by the front door to be loaded into the Volvo on the day of departure was a hand mirror, which we discovered had been broken by the weight of things dumped on top of it. Bill, the only one who could possibly perform the miracle of shoe-horning all this stuff into the car, was stretched pretty taut by this point, and it unsettled him when he saw it.

Cary intervened. Pitch the mirror in the trash, she said. Keep cool, everybody. Instantly and gratefully, we obeyed her. Every now and then, I thought, this family operates like a team. And the leadership often comes from the kids.

Cary has taken charge of all of this college business. All last summer I'd nagged her to work on her college admissions applications, but then one day she just began steaming right through them, pausing only to ask us to write the checks. She seemed to still be at full throttle as she decided among the colleges that admitted her. Her confidence has run high and she believes she has written her own ticket. Well, essentially she has. I doubt she thinks luck has anything to do with the course her life is taking.

If I'm not so sure of that, this is probably not the time to say so. I'm not about to ask a diver, arms raised and on the tips of her toes at the end of the high diving board, whether she has read her horoscope today, either.

The mirror shards in the wastebasket, we went on about our business of stuffing Cary's favorite worldly goods into the car. She is convinced that she will not be homesick, and on that at least, I'll place my wager that she's right.

Bay Head

With the ten-year-old Volvo station wagon so full in the back that you probably could have slid a ball-point pen in there, but not much more, and the carrier that we call The Clam loaded on top, we headed north, planning to break our trip from Virginia to Massachusetts with an overnight stay at my parents' home on the Jersey shore.

David, given the choice of staying with friends in Norfolk and playing in the first soccer tournament of the season, chose to come with us. He is going to miss Cary terribly.

The stay in New Jersey might well strain my already high state of agitation, I thought, and being a daughter the same day I was giving up my own daughter might be a bit much. But convenience and fatigue and a sense of the rightness of passing through the hands of grandparents on the way to college prevailed. We were well received and ate great quantities of the fresh crab that my father catches in traps all summer long.

Cary was magnificent through all this. She has been patient and unflustered—very much in control, choreographing her show on her own terms, and she knows it. Neither broken mirrors nor the possibility that her parents or her grandparents would baby her would deflate her determination.

"How do you think it will feel," my mother asked during dinner, "to do your own laundry?" This apparently innocent question might have carried with it the suspicion that Cary hadn't done her share of household chores over the years.

Detecting the suspicion but impervious to it, Cary said, "Oh, I've been doing the laundry for over a year. No problem." That light and airy dismissive cliché "no problem" sounded wonderful this time.

"You mean your own laundry?" my mother asked.

"No, everybody's laundry," she said, smiling beatifically. And she had. I hadn't considered yet that one of the consequences of Cary's departure was that I'd resume the role of laundry-folder. Or to be realistic, nobody would fold the laundry and it would be every man for himself.

My mother raised an eyebrow. And then she smiled, and she and my father drifted to smoother paths of conversation that carried us into the evening, offering their generosity and expansiveness of spirit to us all, maybe sensing how such a blessing was needed.

After dinner, Cary and David decided to walk to the beach, perhaps a third of a mile away. David took his skateboard, and I tagged along. They have always loved this seaside village, where kids too young to drive can still explore every nook and cranny on foot. They know where you can find magazines or corn to feed the Canada geese, and they know just what is the right time of day to get fresh doughnuts. They especially love the candy store filled with expensive handmade chocolates in glass cases, shoestring red licorice and barley candy, and such rare and exotic finds as candy cigarettes, now nearly extinct.

But the shops were closed by now.

I probably should have let them be with just each other this last night before the commencement of their grown-up separation. But selfishly, I refused to give up an hour of Cary's waning time with us. The two of them scampered and ran ahead of me, alternately using and trying to steal possession of the skateboard, laughing and teasing as if they were no more than six or eight years old.

They visited the beach—it's almost a pilgrim's ritual that whenever we go to Bay Head, even just to pass through town, or in the winter, we must all walk into the edge of the surf, almost as if paying homage to a living and benevolent being that has deigned to give us so much pleasure over the years.

It was nearly dark by now, but we headed back to the house by a longer route, over the canal where we sometimes dangle lines with chicken necks tied to them into the water, to try to catch the crabs that are carried by a leisurely tide in and out of an inland pond. We passed the Episcopal church and the small police station and paused by a carefully tended park with a playground made of heavy timbers. Never an enthusiastic playground-sitter when the children were young, I was nonetheless glad to linger this one last time as they insisted on staying to play on the apparatus in the dark.

Was this a seventeen-year-old about to go to college? A four-teen-year-old lacrosse ace closing in on six feet tall? They climbed and jumped noisily. (Would the police emerge from their station and chase us away?) They pushed each other on the tire swing and played follow-the-leader along the high beam that it hung from. It reminded me of a mature cat who had gotten into the catnip, an old woman hearing the music she had once loved taking to the dance floor again. The climbed up the slide and then slid down it backward and on their stomachs. They ran and chased each other, laughing all the while, completely unself-conscious, natural and innocent, the cover of darkness relieving them of the burden of acting their age.

They have always played together so well, I thought, savoring the times when they had little more to do than play, times slipping away from them now. They have trusted each other, enjoyed each other's confidence. They are bone of each other's bone. And the sweetness of their spending their last night as children together on a playground, as the dark gathered, filled my heart.

The darkness was a blessing to me, too, for I did not want to spoil their joy with the heaviness of heart that kept my own joy company.

Reading Matter

"I stayed up really late, but I finished that stupid book," Cary announced in the car. She must be in training for doing assignments the night before they are due, I thought. She'd been asked to read two or three books in preparation for orientation sessions for incoming students, and this last book was an autobiography of a deaf girl.

"I hate books about life journeys and passages," Cary grumbled.

"Well," I said, "I guess we'll have to differ on that. Those are about the only stories that interest me these days."

I wondered whether the fact that she was in the midst of her own life passage had somehow soured her on other people's. Perhaps there are times when the energy it takes to do great things and stay on an even keel is so prodigious that only later can we think and talk about them. Our prehistoric ancestors may have told those tales of the great hunt only after the beast had been roasted and the community gathered around a fire that had died to embers.

Checks

A dream while I was pregnant with Cary: I awake to the sound of a baby's cry, but I cannot find the baby. Finally, more and more distraught, I follow the cord of a telephone, and as I get closer and closer to the baby, the crying gets louder.

A dream when Cary was about four: I awake in a panic because I have just discovered that I have forgotten to feed my child from all the food groups, and there have been dire and irreversible (but unspecified) nutritional consequences.

At registration in the big gym at Smith College I discover that my child-rearing has indeed missed something important. I failed to instruct Cary in how to keep a checking account. She will now be set loose on the world of personal finance untutored. She missed the Principles of Finance course in high school—a state requirement that had to be waived so that she could take Art History instead—and I didn't fill in the gap. I remember with shame that I haven't reconciled my own checkbook in over twenty years.

I haven't taught her how to cook, either, since she showed little interest. And now I find that I have failed to provide her with her own copy of her health insurance coverage card.

My friend Jane had to explain to her college-bound son how to use an alarm clock. She had woken him up herself for seventeen years.

Why isn't there an exhaustive checklist for parents? How many times have other mothers and fathers wryly noted that it's a shame that babies come without instruction booklets? They let just *anybody* go off and have babies, you know.

But standing there in the gym, about to leave Cary on her own recognizance, to her own devices, with her own resources (and the phrases seem bleaker and bleaker), I have the same panicky feeling I did in the dream where I could not find the baby. My sense of my own failure as a parent mortifies me, and I stand there literally embarrassed, like a dumb actor on a stage who has forgotten her lines and never understood them too well to begin with. It seems as though it's pretty much too late to get it all right now.

The Force

One time this past year I said to Cary in passing, "The Force be with you."

Without missing a beat she responded. Translating the passing of the Peace in church to *Star Wars* language was second nature.

"And also with you."

But she did not want to take the prayer book she had been given for Confirmation to college.

Standing outside Cary's new house (they call them "houses" at Smith instead of "dormitories"), I see that St. John's Church is just across the street. Its rector is the man who months ago said Morning Prayer with me.

"There's St. John's Church," I say to Cary, in between carrying loads up the stairs. "I've met the rector."

"You said that once I was in college, my choices about religion were my own," Cary says.

And so I had.

"Right you are," I say. "But there it is. You know what it's for."

David

We left Northampton hot, late, and rattled to the core. We'd helped Cary move in—bought her a rug and a cabinet that was far more complicated for Bill to assemble than the box said it would be, made a preliminary effort at establishing a checking account and hooking up a computer, and come to think of it, we never had lunch. Tote that barge, lift that bale, haul that big box up to the second floor and down that corridor.

David almost didn't come with us. Space was at a premium in the old Volvo wagon, and his soccer tournament was tempting. The haulers and the toters, though, were terribly glad he came, and I suspected that he knew he needed to be a part of this send-off, if only out of curiosity about where Cary would be. (By extension, of course, what sort of place he might find himself four years hence.) He chose to come, and he chose well.

During the unpacking David decided he would assemble Cary's lamps. We'd forgotten lightbulbs, it seemed, so he and I set off on a quest down Northampton's main street for some. He continued to be helpful and patient—no complaining or begging for fast food. He gently and effectively chastised the three of us when we whined or complained. He even told jokes. I noticed this, and I thanked him.

At the moment of departure it was David who pulled us away. Bill might have lingered another hour trying to stage the perfect good-bye (which this did not turn out to be, even *with* the rug, the cabinet, and the lightbulbs). I might have sat at the curbside and wept.

But David told us to stop sniffling. He wasn't afraid of our grief, nor did he seem jealous of the attention focused on Cary. He did not try to pretend our grief was something else. What he did, though, was salve it.

On the way home in the car he applied his homemade balm in a most extraordinary performance. Fourteen-year-olds can be extremely parsimonious with their interactions with their parents. But in a leap into maturity, a great display of generosity, and an absolutely brilliant diversionary tactic, David announced to the two adults in the front seat who were taking turns quietly sobbing and pretending they weren't, "I'm going to give you a lecture on popular music since Jimi Hendrix and the Grateful Dead."

Plugging his portable CD player into the car cigarette lighter, he instructed his audience of two, "You can ask questions, but when I give examples of what I am saying, I'm not going to play excerpts. It violates the music. You have to listen to the whole song." Yes, sir.

We wended our way through the history of rock 'n' roll as we wended our way south through Connecticut and New York to the Garden State Parkway. We heard about Caribbean influences, distortion pedals, the difference between punk, mainstream alternative, grunge, and ska. We talked about song lyrics and whether they reflect joy or despair, and why. We evaluated guitar-playing skills of different musicians. Before we knew it, an hour and a half had passed. Two hours. I wasn't crying, and neither was Bill.

Life has more or less returned to normal in the household—as normal as it can be without Cary—and David is back listening to music on headphones and saying "whatever" in a dismissive way when he doesn't want to hear what I am saying.

But no matter. At a crucial moment, and for a few hours, he did more than prove he could carry the heaviest load in one trip up two flights of stairs. He had somehow become larger than himself, more David than he usually was, a presence who had been anointed with some remarkable power, a giver of a great gift. He had not behaved in this way to deny our grief, or to focus attention on himself at a time when his sister, who had stolen the show, was now absent. He had not done it to play the jester. I doubt that now he would have much to say at all about why he gave his music lecture.

Sometimes I think we are agents—free agents to be sure—of wisdom, and generosity, and goodness, in ways we can't possibly contrive or carry out of our own power. Call it grace, perhaps, or even the opportunity to be a Christ-bearer. For me, I'll never forget my gratitude for David's lecture on rock 'n' roll as we drove from Massachusetts to New Jersey on one momentous September night.

First Hour

We drove from Plainfield, New Jersey, to South Hadley, Massachusetts, with a full car. No computer in those days, of course, nothing electronic at all, but the same sort of bedspread and extra pillows, piles of clothes, books and toiletries and containers for things as Cary has in her room now. My parents, and probably my brother, helped haul all this stuff upstairs to a second-floor room I had been assigned in an old dormitory at Mount Holyoke College.

I met my assigned roommate, who, defying all probability and statistics in these matters, ended up not only being willing to share a room with me all four years but also being a friend for life. Ginny lives in Pennsylvania, but I see her and her family every so often. I have a portrait in my mind, something like a still photo, of Ginny and me on that day. Our parents met one another, and our brothers I think, and Ginny's little sister. Everyone was civil and friendly, hoping for the best, a little worried. The two girls wanted nothing more than for the families to leave so they could begin their real lives, and if there was any grieving to be done, get it over with.

An hour later, with good-byes said and a little settling-in done, I found myself at Glessie's, a pharmacy with tables in the back where you could order sandwiches and coffee from a small lunch counter. Glessie's became my main study venue for four years, as it turned out. But now I was at Glessie's to buy cigarettes.

I had smoked a bit on the sly my senior year in high school. I had bummed cigarettes from my classmates in the Senior Room, where smoking was permitted. But now that I was at college, my days of sneaking would be over. From day one it would be known by anyone who cared to ask that I was a smoker, and smoke I did, all four years. When I arrived home at Thanksgiving of freshman year, I announced my new status and dared my family to challenge it. They didn't. (I had one hell of a time quitting in later years. But that's another story.)

I find myself wondering now just what Cary did in those first few hours and in the first few weeks after being set loose to make her own decisions, establish what status and what self she wishes to project to her new friends, and wishes to fashion for herself. She will, of course, do as she pleases. But a part of me is more than a little worried. Because my own choices were not all salubrious, and because there is a great deal of opportunity at colleges these days (more so perhaps than back in the 1960s) to choose poorly.

I suppose all in all I didn't go too far off the deep end. But the life I led had its self-destructive side, and smoking was not the whole of it. I remember getting far, far too little sleep, "pulling all-nighters" to complete projects that I should not have put off until the last minute. I remember eating unwisely and getting sick without seeking treatment. People look at me skeptically (and I don't know whether my students or my own children look at me with greater disbelief) when I say that I avoided marijuana, LSD, and all the drugs of choice and experiment in those days, and I did not go in for a life of sexual license as some of my friends did. But I do remember discovering that a prescription drug for menstrual cramps had amphetamine-like properties and would turn an impossible late-night, last-minute composition task into a brilliant exercise in creativity, damn the hangover the next day. I remember bouts with undiagnosed bronchitis and probably pneumonia, when I still dragged myself to classes and even kept smoking. I remember so studiously avoiding exercise that my criterion for selecting courses in the four required semesters of physical education was that no sweating should be involved. (Thus my canoeing, archery, diving, and fencing credentials, such as they are.)

And what about Cary? I wonder where she is, what she is doing, and how well she is caring for herself. I know that there will be no answers for me, that she is in a sense her own mother now. Maybe she is surrounded by friends who will mother her when necessary, and I pray she is being protected by her heavenly Mother. Mostly I harbor a feeble hope that she will have much better sense than I did.

A Map of the World

I almost didn't read *A Map of the World*[2] this summer because I knew it fell into that category I call "dead-baby stories." My old roommate Ginny said to me, "I just can't do it." I take her point. I heard an interview with Jane Hamilton on National Public Radio, and she explained that as a mother she has these terrors too but that her way of taming them is to imagine herself into the unimaginable in gruesome detail so that it won't actually happen. Ginny and I can't pretend that these scenarios of doom do not pay visits to us. Still, I'm not really sure why I read this extraordinary book.

In *A Map of the World* a child's accidental death sets off a chilling series of events, while lives, hopes, respectability, and all that Alice and the other characters in the book have ever hoped to possess unravel and slip out of their grasp.

This disturbing book is about loss, and there was little comfort in its being fiction. I did at first try to talk myself out of identifying with Alice. My children can swim. My neighbors couldn't possibly behave like that. Surely the system of justice would recognize innocence more readily. But what Jane Hamilton does in *A Map of the World* is to gradually, imperceptibly deprive the reader of the comfort of otherness. We are all finally included in the ambit of the inevitability of loss.

---

2. Jane Hamilton, *A Map of the World* (New York: Doubleday, 1994).

In one sweetly painful scene the unjustly jailed Alice, out on bail, is told by her five-year-old daughter that she doesn't want her mother to resume reading to her before bed: She'd rather listen to her tapes. So Alice goes to sleep on the child's floor, listening to the tapes too and remembering listening over and over again to a tape her own mother had made for her before her death.

We may not all be jailed and put on trial like Alice, but all of us will be jilted by our children, all of us will lose our parents in one way or another, and all of us will find ourselves in the agony of aloneness and death in the midst of life, sleeping on the floor so as to be as close as possible to that which we have loved beyond measure and lost.

There is the faintest glimmer of hope at the end of the novel, seen in a child's resilience, a husband's persistence, and Alice's tentative reaching toward compassion and forgiveness. But this book affected me deeply. In a dream the night after I finished the book I was Cary, forgiving a persecutor who had caused me terrible damage. I considered how change and loss are woven into all our lives, and although sometimes we seem so separate from each other and so alone, at other times all our stories seem inextricably bound into one story—so much so that Jane Hamilton's fearful imagination and the fabric of my own life and Cary's are nearly one, and we are of one blood in a universe where all will be taken away, but nothing in fact will be lost.

Chapter 4—A Place in the Nest Is Empty

Watch over your child, O Lord, as her days increase;
bless and guide her wherever she may be.
Strengthen her when she stands;
comfort her when discouraged or sorrowful;
raise her up if she falls;
and in her heart may your peace which passes understanding
abide all the days of her life; through Jesus Christ our Lord. Amen.[1]

Neighbors

Today my next-door neighbor Robin, a generous woman who for years and without complaint has cut the three feet of grass on the other side of our driveway, and who has one child, approached me as I was stepping over this coming winter's half-moved pile of firewood to get to my car. Robin is trim and orderly, and beside her (as beside much of the world, I have to admit) I feel shabby and sloppy, and maybe half-stacked, like the wood. She is a good person, and she came to ask me about Cary.

I have been asked fifty times since coming home from Massachusetts how I am doing, and how Cary is doing. Not just by close friends, either, but by neighbors and people at church, even by my students. They ask earnestly and from the heart, with great

---

1. *The Book of Common Prayer,* 830.

gentleness. I have received a pastoral call from one of the clergy at church. This attention is not just a matter of social courtesy or kindness. People overcome their mild worry that they might be invading my privacy because they really *must find out* (as they might urgently ask, with great concentration and focus, about someone who'd returned from drowning). How does it feel to do this?

I say that on the day we took Cary to Smith, there was an orientation program for students and families that David and Bill slipped out of so they could begin unloading the car. Cary and I endured a rendition of *gaudeamus igitur* that jollied the audience into participation, but I could not bring myself to sing. There were speeches that, in retrospect, were fine, but they barely served to stay my panic. If there had been one false note, one incompetent remark, I might have whisked Cary right back to Virginia. There were none.

At the time, it occurred to me that this was like telling bedtime stories to prisoners about to be tortured. I couldn't sit still. I had trouble paying attention. I felt like a restless two-year-old.

Yet there was a man, a dean I think, who rose to say to the assembled parents, to the assembled coiled springs sitting in auditorium seats: For four or five days you will be distraught and will be beside yourselves with sadness for the loss of your children. But it will pass.

Now just who in the hell, I said to myself, does he think he is? How could anyone presume to predict the course of my grief?

Damn. He was right.

We were home by Sunday, and on Monday I was shopping for a few things in my favorite small grocery store. By the second aisle it dawned on me that I need purchase nothing to accommodate Cary's weird grazing, nearly vegetarian eating style. No bags of raw almonds, no huge quantities of fruits, fresh and dried. No pita bread and hummus. I rounded a corner to aisle three, and who should I see but my friend Lee Ann from church. "How are you doing?" she asked. And right there in the coffee aisle of Gene Walters' Marketplace I burst into tears. Could I say that I was crying because I did not need to buy hummus? Well, considering it was Lee Ann, yes. She has five children, and her last went off to college last year.

Now this is quite interesting. Nobody who has already lost a child to adulthood has considered my grief ridiculous or trivial for even a second. I have been treated—this may seem silly, but I am telling you the truth—as though I have survived the death of a loved one. And those who have suffered the same loss are on an even keel, possessed of a wisdom generated by their having passed this way, but they are in no way condescending. There is a respect, a deep respect. A confraternity of sorrow, but also of transcendence of it, a knowledge of the rightness of it all.

Equally interesting is the response from the people with children younger than Cary, parents like Robin next door, whose children are approaching this rite of passage (as of course all children are). These parents are all the more avidly interested in my narratives, drinking in the details, trying to absorb the nature of my experience as if to keep it on file, yet horrified. It is both as terrible as a science fiction nightmare and as inevitable as waking up in the morning. It will happen to them and they know it.

They want to hear how I am holding up. How Cary feels about college. What the household is like without her. Whether we got her the right computer. If she likes the classes she chose. I tell them that after about five days I stopped bursting into tears. I tell them that Cary was making herself only half an inhabitant of our household during her last year and that both she and we seemed to be obeying some tried and true wisdom we hadn't known was ours, or reading a road map we hadn't known we had at our disposal, almost in the way that a new baby knows how to announce it is hungry and a new mother knows how to honor the demand even if she hasn't read all the manuals.

I tell them that I miss seeing her and hearing her voice. I say that I miss having her friends call on the phone and congregate in our den, because I enjoyed them so much. But I say that I am surprised at my own calm. My loss is large and textured with many feelings and thoughts, but it is far from unendurable. It is even tinged with a relief that I have been through a dark tunnel that I will not have to transit again—other dark tunnels, of course, but at least not this one again. There is even a sense of the essential rightness of it. Do I feel "older and wiser"? Well, I guess so.

I also know a feeling of gratitude so large I nearly fall on my knees. Grateful to whom? Well, to Smith College, I suppose, for doing its job well, all the way down to putting the right people at the microphones during that orientation program. To Cary for choosing it, and for taking charge of the application process to the point that she is determined to be happy and successful. To Bill's employer, Virginia Wesleyan College, for making it possible for her to get the scholarship that made Smith affordable. To Maury High School and the Norfolk Public Schools for preparing her so well that Smith welcomed her with open arms. And to God's abundant mercy. Few people have it this easy, I suspect. I feel almost elated sometimes, while still carrying the grief on my back. Does that make any sense at all?

I am writing all this because the questions and the conversations in church, in grocery lines, and even with students who barely know me but who are also parents, suggest to me that we are all following a common path—a broad one with different kinds of terrain, but all going in the same direction. We are all brothers and sisters in this—the parents, the children, the neighbors. For us to hold one another's hands as we walk along is about all I ever need to know of blessing on this earth. We hear one another's stories, and we honor them, and we might as well acknowledge that we're all related.

So, how am I doing? Well, I feel like someone who has recovered quite nicely from some radical surgery to remove, say, a left leg. I'm getting around quite well, thank you, and for long periods of time I forget to pay attention to the operation or its results. Every once in a while I think to myself, "Damn, that's right! I don't have my left leg! I'll never have it again!" Briefly, a wave of mourning rushes over me, but then I move on. And it really is not like losing a leg, anyway. There is rightness and goodness in it all, and I know that I'll realize eventually that the correct response is to rejoice.

Concerned Parents Crave Message

Okay, it's very early Monday morning, and she has an eight o'clock Monday-Wednesday-Friday class. But if I call her and she's in a hurry, she'll be furious. If I call her and she's *not there* I'll panic. All this because she has gone three days without answering her e-mail. I know people who go a month without checking their e-mail. But Cary isn't like that. On the other hand, she may have gone away for the weekend. But where would she have gone? Would she have told us?

Oh, how I wish I had the phone number of the other girl from Norfolk who is on Cary's hall. But to call her would be a breach of trust, perhaps. Excessive behavior that would embarrass Cary.

I am sitting on that cusp of indecision, with hysterical fear off to one side and the certainty that I am being a silly fool on the other. I compromise and send an e-mail whose subject line is CON-CERNED PARENTS CRAVE BRIEF MESSAGE. Will you send back a message saying your head is above water? I ask. Three hours later the note comes back; I'm fine, just busy.

I am indeed a silly fool.

The meter of my anxiety leaves the warning zone and gradually swings back into the normal range. For now.

The Care Package

David helped me carry a few packages into the post office the other day. One of them was for Cary. It contained a videotape of an *X-Files* episode for her collection, a sweater she had left behind, some candy and toiletries, and a Chap Stick with Batman on top—she's always loved these little trashy cultural artifacts. As I packed all this stuff in the box and strapped it with clear packing tape, it occurred to me that something was missing.

David hadn't made even the least suggestion that I should buy him an equivalent measure of treats.

Come to think of it, he hasn't made such a suggestion the whole time she's been gone. Is it just that he has my exclusive attention at home and has managed to get me to buy him new lacrosse shoulder pads and other sports gear lately? I think there's more to it.

When David was born, I remember thinking very carefully about how to introduce Cary, then nearly four, to this new creature who would muscle her out of the center of attention and physical nurturing. It might be clever, I thought, to try to treat the baby in a rather businesslike way in front of her, while saving the cuddly, fond behavior for when she wasn't there, to prevent jealousy. Find special occasions, one of the advice books said, to be alone with the older child when the new baby's needs will not take precedence. I considered this.

But I followed a different instinct, which was to talk with Cary about this and to tell her that babies certainly did require a great deal of attention and work and physical closeness such as nursing and diaper changes. But all this had to be done with love and gentleness, and this was exactly how I had treated her. She now had the chance to be a caregiver too, since she'd both received it and now knew how it was done.

This turned out to be the right formula for Cary, and David was certainly the beneficiary. We even have a photo of David at a music festival on the Elizabeth River in downtown Norfolk on a warm fall evening. David is lying on his back on a blanket with his head turned to one side, contentedly sucking Cary's thumb, which she has proudly offered.

People ask David what it's like to have his four years as an "only child" in his teens—is it better for him than it was for Cary, who can hardly remember enjoying it in her first four years? An impossible question to answer, of course. But all these years their rivalry has been minimal, perhaps because it seemed best to lavish the attention and not keep it secret. If so, it means that David is now learning what Cary did back then: that when he is seventeen not only will we buy him a computer but he too will be allowed to go to a college far away from home, he too will be trusted to be in charge of much of his own life, and he too will receive packages filled with goodies and tokens of the abiding need of mom and dad to lavish attention and favor on one so beloved.

The American Revolution

So, I am standing in an American History classroom this fall semester trying to explain that Edmund Burke was a wise man and that if King George III and his Tories had listened carefully to Burke's advice, we might still be singing "God Save the Queen" over here in the colonies at the beginning of the World Series.

As a member of Parliament and a Whig, Burke gave a blistering speech in 1775 chastising the British government for its idiocy in trying to bind the Empire by force and to threaten the American colonies into continued loyalty. Do you have such weak imaginations, he asks his opponents in the House of Commons, that you think this glorious Empire is bound together as one by bonds, affidavits, and sufferances? Do you think that the bravery of our great army is a result of existing penalties for mutiny? No, he says. Bravery and loyalty can be assured only if the people love England and derive advantage from being English. What binds the Empire, in fact, is *love*. As the American colonies mature, their love can be sustained only if they are more and more free to order their own affairs and are permitted their freedoms, looking over their shoulder to a mother country with whom association is more and more voluntary all the time.

I paused, and as so often happens while I am standing in front of a class, an analogy popped into my mind from out of the blue. Suppose when you raise your children, I said, that you compel their good behavior by the threat of dire punishment. If you eat cookies for breakfast or pull the cat's tail, you will be spanked five times! If you skip school or smoke cigarettes behind the garage, you will be grounded for a week! Suppose that their ties to home and family are ties of fear or hurt or loss. Suppose they see you as only the source of rules and sanctions, arbitrary ones whose legitimacy they have never acknowledged and in whose devising they have had no part. Suppose this all has nothing to do with love but only control and the parents' advantage.

What ties will there be once your children reach their majority?

The students all scoffed. There will be no ties at all of value, their gestures said. The parents will lose.

What Burke understood, I said, was that only if the American colonies believed that they owed their prosperity and their freedoms to their connection with England could the Empire survive. Military compulsion was unnecessary if the ties were by love, useless if there was no love. In fact, England's ability to maintain the Empire by force began to disintegrate the minute the colonists put three thousand miles of ocean between themselves and the mother country. Which is to say about 1607.

I too, I said, have sent my daughter to Massachusetts, as the king of England once sent his countrymen to "New England." How long, I said, may I suppose that I can control her behavior, if it is by curfews and sanctions that I impose by force? Can I tell her when to be in at night or how to eat? Can I remind her to do her homework every evening or limit her TV time?

Smiles broke out on faces around the room, knowing smiles.

Shouldn't my strategy now be to find that I admire what she is and trust her to exercise her freedom? Shouldn't I now praise her for making her own decisions and honor the directions she will take even when they surprise me?

Was I ever as much in control of who she would become as I might have thought?

Can I in any real manner (other than refusing to pay her tuition) command her behavior or be in charge of our relationship? Surely I must now realize that our ties are now voluntary and ordered by affection. I think if I believe otherwise, I am a fool.

I did have the class's attention, and some of the eighteen-year-olds were nodding knowingly. I wonder whether they were thinking about England and the impending American Revolution, or their own mothers and fathers and the ties that were looser and looser all the time.

A New Person

So, what reputation had she forged for herself so far? She seems to have become known for this:

1. She has a television and a VCR. She bought this combined piece of video equipment with her summer earnings. She says that she keeps her room fairly clean, because she has people watching *X-Files* with her.

2. She has not only connected and installed her own computer and printer but she also has helped other people in her house connect theirs. She has been called upon to troubleshoot when computers are malfunctioning.

3. She has become known as the campus-wide expert on *X-Files,* and on science fiction in general. Word has it that January-term classes can be taught by students, if proposals for them are good enough. She is cooking up a scheme to teach a weeklong January term course next year on *X-Files,* the fear of the alien, and American popular culture.

4. She is known as an artist and has done caricatures of her housemates, depicting them as versions of the characters on the cartoon TV program *South Park.* These cartoons are posted on people's doors.

A young woman named Karen, whose parents are neighbors of ours, was in our living room this past summer trying to sell us a set of knives. It was her summer job after her freshman year at Princeton, and she promised that if we would tolerate her sales pitch, we would not have to make any purchases, since she was paid even for making the demonstration. We did end up buying some knives. I can never resist buying Girl Scout cookies, either.

Anyway, Karen said that she was happy with her first year of college. She had gone to a local private academy, where she had the same classmates, year after year after year. "The main problem," Karen said, "was that everybody knew who you were, both the teachers and the students, and because you never were a stranger, you never had a chance to be a new person. For twelve years."

My friend Foy, who lives in Alabama, says that her daughter, now in graduate school, told her that one of the most important things about going away to college was that she could be herself, Ari, without being her mother and father's daughter. She had hastened to explain, kind child that she was, that she had no objection to the reputation that her mother and father had established for her; in fact, it had opened all sorts of doors. But she had to go forth in the world as nobody's child, nobody's relative or protégée, to find out who she really was.

As I consider Cary's reputation at Smith, I remember her essay about Halloween, and I wonder what costume she may be trying on today.

Dear Cary

We are thrilled to learn that you got all the classes that you wanted. I haven't heard a whisper of a bit of gossip or news from any of your friends, except the Internet ones whose messages I've forwarded to you.

Did you leave behind/lose a tiny thin silver twisted ring? I don't think it's from a cereal box. It's more sturdy. It fits my pinky and it reminds me of you, so I've been wearing it. But I'd be happy to send it to you.

I hope that your cold is much better. Get enough sleep, dear. I'm proud of you for how you are conquering your new world, and Northampton looks like a town worth conquering.

We love you.

Love,

Mom

You know those fascinating pictures by Escher where on the far right of the canvas you have a school of fish or something, and by the middle of the canvas you have a flock of birds flying west, and at the extreme left of the canvas, you have, maybe, butterflies? You see the transition before your very eyes, but you can't put your finger on just exactly where fish becomes bird. There's a play between positive and negative space, and the adroitness of it leaves you smiling but quite a bit off balance.

We are in that transition ourselves, the Jones family, where Cary is of this household and of this organism of a family. She comes from here and she is of our flesh. There was a time when all that she experienced and knew, I knew that she knew. Much of it I taught her. But then she went to preschool and elementary school, and she came home chirping away about children I hadn't met and events I hadn't witnessed. At first, when she was four or five, she didn't realize that the life she lived out of my presence would be something I didn't know about. Soon she grasped this. Soon afterward, she understood the precious nature of this fact, and she began to know herself as a person distinct from the family, even while within it. She understood the preciousness of being able to share what she chose to share.

The Escher progression had begun.

Now is the great transformation. By the end of college, she will see herself as no more than a visitor in the home that gave her birth. She will carry that pattern with her forever, but it will be as if it is the negative image rather than the positive one. What was once fish anchored in these waters has become a bird in flight. Where once we knew everything about her world, it is more and more true that we know of her world what she wishes to tell us.

If psychologists wish to call it individuation, I understand. I was recently asked by a psychologist in a group exercise to draw my family. I drew a green spiral with Bill and me at the center, but the spiral does not have closed edges on its outer rim; the family has a permeable membrane, for people to go in and out, for the breath of spirit to go in and out. At the outer edge of the spiral, I drew two gracefully protruding semi-spheres—a large one for Cary, a less developed one for David. They look a bit like cells dividing, or droplets about to depart from the mother water source. Soon they will put space between themselves and their host. I colored them with all the colors of the rainbow, like those beautiful rising hot-air balloons, as they lift themselves from the confinement of earth's gravity. As fish becomes bird.

And somehow this is the most beautiful and right thing I know of, and the scar it leaves as the new life is born is a great honor to sustain.

October Weekend

Cary is coming home tomorrow for her first visit since she went away, and I am on edge. Bill says to clean the house. The house normally isn't clean; we don't want her to feel ill at ease, I say. It's special, he says, I want her to feel honored. I remember how small and dingy my house seemed the first time I came home from college. All right.

My neighbor and friend Beth says ominously, Cary will come home, but it'll never be the same. Beth has been through this before.

She is right, of course. I warn Bill that I remember my first visit home from college. I announced that I was a smoker, and I behaved like an obnoxious know-it-all. We must prepare ourselves, I say, to be treated as if we were clods and rubes. As if we had no right to question her comings and goings or to place demands on her time and attention. Our job is to be impressed with and embrace the new Cary, who with any luck will not have dyed her beautiful red-blonde hair and will have not pierced anything else. We must not get rattled.

I am feeling rattled.

Yesterday, three little messages scraped at the smooth edges of my composure. First, my neighbor Lilian who had both her children stay in town for college—one of them living at home until gradua-tion—asked me how Cary is. I said that she seemed extremely pleased with herself and her situation. Is she homesick? Strangely no, I said, I haven't heard the least hint of homesickness. (If Cary *were* homesick, I thought, I think she would conceal it from both me and herself, so set is she on this course of her own choosing.)

Lilian's daughter Sarah is homesick, she said, away from home for the first time. We stood there sizing each other up, no doubt both shifting back and forth between defensiveness and anxious guilt about our mothering. Have I done a great job because Cary has gone so confidently out in the world that she has so far not called us on the phone once? Or have I been such a negligent mother, maybe an oppressive mother, that she insisted on going to college in another state and likes it? Has Lilian been a better mother because she successfully shielded both children from the treacherous pitfalls that college life offers kids today? Has she created such a happy home that her grateful and admirably sensible children delayed their departure until their majority? I wonder what Lilian was thinking, standing as we both were in front of the potatoes and onions in our neighborhood mom 'n' pop grocery store. It was such a complicated moment that we stood silent for many seconds without realizing that conversation had failed.

Then, in a book I'm reading by Bennett Sims about "servant leadership" I saw a phrase in passing about abused children leaving home early. What was that? Should I have put up a greater resistance to Cary's going nearly six hundred miles away to college? Did I make home something to escape rather than to cling to?

Or could it be that children are different: some fly, some cling?

Then, late at night, Cary responded to my e-mail about whether she had a way to get to the airport in the morning. *I'm getting on the bus (ticket: 28 bucks, wanna pay me back? I'd just as soon stay here) at 5:35 A.M. to get to Bradley by 7:45, and then I have to hang around until 9:10 when my flight is. Life sucks. If you leave me for an hour at the airport like last time, I'm getting on a plane and coming right back here. I'm missing a trip to New York with Dawn for this. Please pick me up, okay?*

Ah, the rehearsal of old grievances, like last summer's late pickup from the airport after the Italy trip. The solicitation of $28. The broad suggestion that this whole trip is of our devising, not hers, and that she is doing us a difficult favor. The rather cheerful verbal combat. The plea to be picked up. Sounds like all is well to me.

I threw up my hands and went to bed. I'll clean the house tomorrow. A little.

October Weekend Epilogue

She slept until after noon. She spent much of the time on the computer. And she slept through part of church. At dinner at a favorite restaurant, she told stories and answered questions. She really is the old Cary, and our relief is overwhelming and sweet.

I thanked her for coming home, for our sake, and for David's. Your next three October weekends are all your own, I said. We'll see you at Thanksgiving.

Movie Review

Cary's e-mail was about a movie that Bill and I also saw, *L.A. Confidential*. Cary sees ten times as many movies as we do, and all of them before us. Cary and Bill loved this one, and I didn't. I am often the odd man out. Why like a movie that is utterly nihilistic, I say, even if it is imaginative and stylish? I know postmodern fun when I see it, and I'm not a total prude, but the bloodiness of this movie and the hollowness of its core alternately bored and repelled me.

"I've never respected Mom's movie choices before; why should I start now?" her message to Bill asked.

You have to kill the mother, I remember my priest friend Win once put it.

Bill has been such a good father to Cary, and in so many ways, they think alike. When she was a newborn, he would carry her on his shoulder and sing old forties' numbers to her into the early hours of the morning, until she would finally give in to sleep. He remembers singing her to sleep during the blizzard of 1980 in Norfolk, walking in the dark living room watching the snow fall softly by streetlight. He's been the sentimental one, and they share a great devotion to movies. No one could imagine a better daddy.

Over these seventeen years I've done a good deal of what I call kid maintenance—keeping up with Cary's and David's schedules and transportation needs, going to parent-teacher conferences, helping edit papers and struggle through research for science projects, buying and hemming and washing their clothes, shopping for obscure vegetarian foods and art supplies and books, filling Christmas stockings, driving to club meetings and practices and doctors' appointments, paying the bills, and laying down, then amending rules. I've usually maintained an emotional barometer that doesn't swing too widely off the scale, because that's how I'm made. Parenting rewards those with nerves of steel, that's for sure. And most recently, I have helped prepare for this great leap into going to college.

You know, I'm just getting cranked up with this list, and I could easily be drilling a hole down which I might crawl with some self-righteous self-pity that could close me in. How ridiculous that would be.

The fact is that all this mothering was not done begrudgingly or by way of piling up credits or counting cost, any more than in those first months I resented giving Cary milk or counted that the giving of it in any way diminished me.

Could I ever thank my mother for her milk? For her nurturing or for the list that she might be able to prepare of the things she did for me? Well, at my age I probably ought to give it a try. But I can never know the extent of her loving, can only imagine it by observing my own loving of my two children, celebrate it by passing it down to the next generation.

It is probably good not to be burdened with too much of a debt of gratitude until you are old enough to realize that the giving of life to your child fulfills rather than diminishes. A child held hostage to a price ticket of gratitude cannot grow strong and true. I have known people crippled and hobbled by needy parents who hold their children with ties of guilt and obligation. It is a loving thing to forgo being needy.

There is another dimension to it. If my mother had that capacity to love me beyond human measure and in ways I could not then perceive or measure, and if I have had that same capacity to love Cary and David, surely then I can suppose that I am loved even more extravagantly by a God who allows us to forget sometimes the divine source of the love, but prefers that we turn to those others who need that love to flow downward, without the bill being presented.

Do I crave gratitude or expressions of devotion? I would prefer that Cary pass it along, in who she is and what she does, in ways I mostly will never see.

But then again, we have a late-night e-mail exchange, which ends like this:

Me: *Oof. I've been up since 4:15 this morning. I think I need to wander upstairs for a hot bath.*

Cary: *Heh. It's 4:37 A.M. and I'm just GOING to bed. I love you too, and you don't need to doubt your ability to parent or the fact that I trust you. And now I'm going to sleep. :-)*

love cary

P.S. Tell Dad that I'm focusing my American Graffiti/Last Picture Show *paper on revisiting a past that can't be revisited—both in the context of the 1960s and the characters themselves. In other words, I'm saying that the films show that you can never go back to the way things used to be in a simpler and easier time.*

Cats, Mothers

When Cary was ten or eleven, she brought home a tiny new kitten from the animal shelter and named him Colley. Colley was, as it turned out, very sick. Cary held him by the hour and fed him with a dropper. He soon died. You could hold him in the palm of your hand. The vet advised us to wait a while before bringing a new animal into the house, lest vestiges of the distemper from the one cat infect the next. Later, Cary got Henry, a healthy, wonderful cat who lived long and had a terrific personality.

When her brother, David, was very little, Cary would invent games for him and would award him prizes—a deck of cards, a Lego person, a funny hat. She'd wrap the prize elaborately, and it was the receiving of the prize from Cary, rather than the item itself, that pleased him most.

For his part, David was keenly aware of Cary's frame of mind and very protective of her when she was hurt. If she was in distress he would bring his cherished blanket and apply it, like a nurse applying a clean dressing to a wound, to whatever part of her seemed most in need. Then he would lay his head on her and lean quietly for a moment.

Once Henry disappeared and was gone for several days. Cary was disconsolate. She made posters with a drawing and description of the cat, and our phone number. We nailed posters to telephone poles and trees, and we said prayers for Henry's safety and his return. She was sure he would be found. I was not so sure.

About five days later, a college student who lived more than a mile away called to ask where we lived. He was pretty sure his new stray cat was Henry, and he wanted to bring him back to Cary. It indeed was Henry, and the prodigal was returned.

We got an e-mail from Cary last night saying that she had the flu and was very, very miserable. With a distress that I felt physically in my own body, I realized that I cannot mother Cary from six hundred miles away. Can she mother herself? Dare I hope that among her new friends there is someone with a history of nurturing brothers and cats who will take adequate care of her?

As college is in every respect the great divide between childhood and adulthood, I suppose that we need to learn to mother and be mothered by a larger circle of people than those to whom we are related. It's hard for me to relinquish that job, but I suppose I see that family is as family does. A child who can be so devoted to a cat and a brother as Cary has been is well on the road to knowing what devotion really is.

Six A.M.

For years I've done it. I set my alarm for either five or six, depending on which day of the week it is and what my work schedule is. On the six o'clock days I notice that somewhere between one minute before to one minute after the alarm goes off—with no more variation than that—someone who lives around the corner and just out the bedroom window on my side of the bed starts up a car with a defective muffler or no muffler at all, warms it up for a couple of minutes, then heads off past my house, to work, I suppose. There are a number of odd things about this. One is that I can't imagine that his muffler passes the state car inspection, and it has sounded like this for far more than a year. Another is that I have never actually met either the car owner or anyone else who lives in that house, unusual for this friendly neighborhood. I suppose, moreover, that I'm only guessing that the owner is a man. Nor could I pick the car out of a lineup—by sound I could do it, but not by sight.

I have been musing on this unknown neighbor who is so utterly regular in his habits and who has apparently had exactly the same job, year after year after year. I must say, I admire his faithful behavior, and I marvel that he thrives on such predictability. But I found myself thinking this morning, as I deliberately lay in bed for five more minutes lest I be so predictable myself, how mysterious it is that we end up in certain occupations and not others.

Cary said last night on the phone that she would register for the second semesters of Art and Italian and add both another class in film and one in American Studies. If I were to guess what major she will choose, I'd put my money on American Studies with a minor in Film. I remember that thirty-two years ago I was deflected from my original choice of college major by a single sentence at a crucial moment, so I shall marshal all my will to keep from interfering with Cary's decision.

But thinking about these choices, these steps we take at one moment that draw us down this path or that path, to the exclusion of the other one, and thinking of the man who leaves for his job promptly at six year after year, I wonder about this business of calling and vocation: the strange story of how we all come to be where we are.

A few weeks ago Cary enthusiastically reported on her job as an assistant to a professor, a scholar of early television, and her course in the history of film. "I can't believe they call this work!" she said. "I need to find something to do with my life that is this much fun!"

And indeed, that is exactly the task. I have told her more than once: Find the calling where you can't believe they actually pay you to have so much fun, where you do prodigious amounts of work and can still rejoice at the end of the day.

So many of my own students say to me, "I love history, but I can't get a job in it. I know that there are jobs in accounting, so I guess I'll do that." I am gentle and indirect with them, but I want to climb up on my swivel office chair and proclaim from a great height with arms outstretched, "This is your *life* we are talking about here! Where is your *joy*? Don't settle for something that *Money* magazine tells you is a safe career!"

Have I followed my own bliss, as Joseph Campbell would put it? Well, that's a whole 'nother story, isn't it? Trouble is, the call can be different at different times in your life. Or maybe what was murky at twenty-five is now very clear at fifty. While middle age gives you clarity and has given me a stronger and stronger conviction that there are "vocations" that are actually the voice of God at work rather than mere "career choices," it is cruelly true that the further down one path you go, the more difficult it is to leave it behind for another.

My prayer for Cary is that she will follow the voice that lures her with true bliss, because I'm quite convinced that God speaks to us through our joy far more than through our dread or even our good sense. Perhaps I will even include in my prayer the man whose name I do not know but whose regular presence at dawn on his way to his work is somehow both a mystery and a comfort along the way.

Home Sweet Home

Journal entry, April 30, 1988

(Cary is eight, David is four and a half.)

Cary is out on an overnight—at a birthday party on a friend's family houseboat. David was crushed that she was leaving. I took him on an after-dinner bike ride as consolation. Very soon he will be too old to ride on the back of my bicycle in the child seat. As we got home and darkness fell, David said that he didn't think he'd be able to sleep tonight. "Cary is the nicest girl in the universe," he said. Coming in the back door he stopped and said reflectively, "Home Sweet Home just isn't Home Sweet Home if Cary isn't here."

David would never remember he ever said that, but the other day, with his sister now at college, he said out of the blue, "God, I miss Cary."

He may be remembering those games Cary made up for him, and the wrapped prizes, and the consolation when she was sad. Surely he is remembering times when they depended on each other that I know nothing about.

They talk on the phone these days, and when they do, they seem to talk forever. David talks on the phone too with his friends— boys, and quite a number of girls too. He treats the girls with respect and attention, and he may be receiving back some care that is a new version of what his sister used to supply.

Little Cross

The e-mail arrived. *"You know the little gold cross you gave me for my sixteenth birthday? It's either in my jewelry box with the little drawers, or in the Fossil watch tin. Please send. Hurry. The little silver ring I left behind? You can do anything you want with that."*

My heart warmed at the prospect that the little cross mattered to her. Perhaps she needed its comfort. Did I dare hope that God had somehow spoken into her ear?

I e-mailed her back the next day. *"Cross packaged up and on its way. Do you have special plans for it?"* My own hopefulness was so pathetic it actually made me laugh. Cary's soul will be just fine, I know it.

The answer came three days later. *"Thanks for the package. I'm glad it came by this weekend. It's part of my Halloween costume. I'm Dana Scully. And I've dyed my hair."*

The heroine of *X-Files* always wears a small gold cross, and her hair is much redder than Cary's.

I've been wearing the silver ring on my little finger, and it makes me feel much better, almost all the time.

Chapter 5—Branching Out

Heavenly Father, we thank you that by water and the Holy Spirit
you have bestowed on this your servant the forgiveness of sin,
and have raised her to the new life of grace.
Sustain her, O Lord, in your Holy Spirit,
Give her an inquiring and discerning heart,
the courage to will and to persevere,
a spirit to know and to love you,
and the gift of joy and wonder in all your works. Amen.[1]

Branching Out

We saw Smith for one day and have a snapshot of it in our minds. Cary has been there for three months, and she has explored a living and breathing town that's far from static or frozen in a picture frame. She has found all sorts of places that she likes: places to see movies and to buy snacks and daily necessities. She knows the shopkeepers and the businesses; she knows what she does and doesn't like. I assume that she has learned to navigate what to me seem incredibly baroque and dangerous traffic patterns in downtown Northampton. She's met dozens and dozens of people and has found new friends that we haven't met. She has, I hope, learned

---

1. The prayer for the newly baptized. *The Book of Common Prayer*, 308.

where the best places are to study, how to comfort herself when she is under stress, and how to protect herself from what might hurt her.

She can't wait until her birthday in November, she says, because you can't get a card to rent movies unless you're eighteen. But she's found the college's video library, where she can check out mostly very old movies and take them back to her room to watch, and a shop where the owner loves to talk about movies with college students.

What she knows of her new life in Northampton, we catch only fleeting and faint glimpses of, only as much as her e-mail messages convey of it. Only what she has time to tell; only what she wishes to tell. And so it will be from now on.

She has grown in these three months as much as she grew the first three months out of my womb, learning to deal with a whole new world, growing off the trunk of the tree into being her own branch. I suppose my job is to be the trunk, changing in a more stately and less visible manner, providing stability and predictability. Her branch is growing fast, stretching out, producing new shoots and the promise of lovely flowers, reaching for the sky, and only connected to the trunk and to the ground by the basest of necessities, the most ignorable of practicalities.

And as for Cary, home for her may be a snapshot frozen in time too.

November

I was taking a bath tonight, and I was so startled that I dropped the soap with a splash into the water. I had not thought of Cary yet today. Can sadness and sweet and rich rightness be woven into one blessed moment?

Nancy

I met Nancy on the Internet quite a while ago, and in person last April when Cary and I went to Massachusetts to visit Smith and Mount Holyoke. We had coffee together in Northampton while Cary was being wooed by one of the colleges. I liked Nancy as much in real life as I did by e-mail, and I figured that if Cary saw a sign that Smith was the right place for her next four years, there was no reason I couldn't take Nancy as my own personal sign.

For one thing, she makes me feel that there is a real mom in Northampton if Cary needs one. Cary's had no such need so far. But I've been the one who's needed Nancy to be there—just in case. Nancy tells me what the weather is like and what she and her dog, Jonah, see when they take walks on the Smith campus. She even told me that it was Mountain Day early that morning—that's the day when classes are unexpectedly called off so everyone at all five local colleges can enjoy a beautiful fall day outdoors, hiking or picnicking or exploring. I e-mailed Cary to have a nice Mountain Day and enjoyed her surprise and confusion that I was so mysteriously well informed.

Nancy also will let Bill and me stay in her guest room when we bring and fetch Cary these four years. Like us, she and her husband are college teachers and parents. I think back with gratitude on my great discovery almost eighteen years ago that one of the true blessings of parenthood is that it is impossible to survive it without help.

If the Internal Revenue Service could actually manage to catch all of us barterers, all of us who've traded services in taking care of one another's small children and failed to pay taxes on the value of services received, they could eradicate the national debt. I cannot count high enough to calculate the number of times I've been instructed or comforted by parents who have experienced one mothering trial or another, just one step ahead of my experiencing it.

My latest benefactor is Nancy, and I'll never be able to pay her back. My mind is set to rest simply because she is there. Back home in Norfolk, an old friend from twenty years ago has given our phone number to her son, who is stationed here in the Navy. Just in case, of course.

Meanwhile, Nancy says that Northampton's first snow is predicted for this weekend. I think I'll tell Cary that the package with the heavy sweaters is on its way.

Psalm

Her e-mail came late at night: there was a suicide in one of the houses—it was a girl Cary didn't know, a junior. It was the only message I have received so far that has been less than cheerful and triumphant. Smith College may never have seen a first-year student so determined to be happy. But for a few hours at least, her world was turned upside-down.

This news seems to have affected my equanimity far more than hers. To be a parent has been to consider the unthinkable—the death of my child. It makes contemplating my own death pale in comparison, and it renders the world a far more dangerous place than it ever seemed before. Worse still perhaps, the line between the two children who are mine and the numberless children that other women have given birth to has blurred, and my fears are for all of them. My sense of who is family has somehow expanded to deny even boundaries of acquaintance. Just as I hope that there are many fathers and mothers who will watch over Cary when she needs them, so too all children are mine by adoption.

Before I went to bed I prayed for the child who took her own life, the beloved and infinitely valuable child of parents whose grief just now I cannot possibly imagine, and for all children and parents in this world, where to love is to be vulnerable to suffering that passes all contemplation.

Only half awake early the next morning, I heard this psalm arise within me.

Your children cry out, O God,
Our children cry out in their places of higher education:
We hear their voices of despair in Charlottesville and Berkeley,
In Northampton and Atlanta and Williamsburg;
But they do not know to cry to you.

We hear the children cry in their despair, O God,
To wealth and success for their salvation,
To the accumulation of the things of this world.
Self-fulfillment has become their god,
And they exploit each other on their paths towards adulthood.
They put their faith in entertainment instead of true knowledge,
And blunt their pain with chemicals
That greedy predators are only too willing to supply.
They lie on their lonely beds and begin to ask,
Why is there no meaning in the Universe?

Save the children, O Christ.
Go to them in their places of growing up
And their places of learning.
Be as a still small voice to them in their dormitory rooms as dawn
*   steals up on darkness.*
Teach them through their English classes and their philosophy texts
That love outshines greed and hope conquers despair;
Through their art and music texts that beauty abides though
*   cheapness and exploitation go down to the Pit;*
Through their science and math classes that your mighty presence
*   is manifest in the cell and the number and the vast reaches*
*   where Mir and Challenger go;*
Through their history and political science investigations that you
*   deign to be with us in human society, in the places of power, and*
*   in our very own lives.*

Be present, blessed Holy Spirit, with our children.
Breathe your life into theirs while they play or while they read or
*   while they sleep,*
And make them strong and hopeful, dwelling under the arm of
*   your Love.*
Speak to them from their computer screens and in their laboratories,
On their playing fields and subtly between the lines of their poems;
Yea, perhaps even in their music.
Make them not afraid to whisper the least small syllable to bring
*   you nigh to them,*
In all the healing, all the intelligence, and all the sweetness of
*   your salvation.*
Save them from the snares of this world,
Yet make them strong to contend in this world.
We their mothers and fathers are far away from them,
But as our faith is in you, draw the faith of our children to you too,
That we may be your people from this generation to the next.

Periodicals and Things

These are the two magazines and the two catalogs that Cary
could not live without in her first semester: *Entertainment Weekly*
and the *New Yorker*; Victoria's Secret and J. Crew.

These are some of the things we sent her in care packages: stamps,
Chap Stick, bubble gum, deodorant, blank videotapes, a Day-Glo
toothbrush, microwave popcorn, colored bobby pins, funky socks,
a pack of thank-you notes, camera film, Necco wafers, weird pens
and pencils, rolls of quarters in plastic M & M containers just the

size of a roll of quarters, Post-its, and interesting junk mail.

A Good Time to Die

Reynolds Price's autobiography, *Clear Pictures: First Loves, First Guides,* concludes with an exceedingly moving description of his father's death while Price was a junior at Duke University. The father and son were very close; in fact, in many ways, Price saw that his own life had been bought by his father's personal transformation and bargain with God. As Will Price entered into that vortex of illness, diagnosis, surgery, and decline, he asked for the presence and support of the son he called "Preacher."

Clear Pictures is one of those autobiographies I admire the most: that are a portrait of not only a life but also a soul. Oddly, though, as I read the book, I found myself identifying more with the father than the son. Instead of focusing on what Price offers, which is the experience of losing his father, I found myself wondering whether it would be all right for me to die once both Cary and David are in college.

This whole matter of death has shifted considerably for me since the moment I became a mother. I have to say—and I think I am being honest—I simply never worried much about death before I was thirty-two years old. This no doubt was the twin product of that adolescent conceit that the future stretches to a horizon immeasurably far away, and a faith that immortality, however impossible to envision, was a promise that would be fulfilled according to God's wisdom and benevolence.

But beginning with pregnancy and that dream about not being able to locate the crying baby, I began to develop anxieties about my babies' death and my own. I have imagined unspeakable horrors befalling Cary and David in the here and now and as they grow up. I have cried at newspaper stories about battered children. I refuse to allow the Kingston Trio's old song "Scarlet Ribbons" to be played in my hearing. No dead-baby stories, I say, as if keeping all this outside the circumference of my attention would make it go away.

Once Cary was born I began to consider my own death as well, and how long my children needed me to stay alive. Practically speaking, this two-income family needed more life insurance. Declining term policies were supposed to be the thriftiest and most responsible choice. We chose. But at what point could we allow the curve to decline? For how long would the children be dependent on my motherly care? For how long would they be dependent on my income? How much money (I almost coolly considered this) would it take to replace me?

I thought for the first time not just what my death would mean to Bill in terms of the loss of our love and companionship, our lives woven together, but how he could possibly handle single parenthood?

With these dark thoughts churning around in me, I happened to begin reading Reynolds Price. At twenty-one, he faced his dying father and said to himself, "I am living through this, and I am still standing upright." He stayed at his father's side to the end and then said to himself, "For nearly three weeks I'd been a man, a certified adult. . . . I was lasting, faithful, and dauntless. What else could a father be for but this, to teach such skills? . . . My father had led me to do a large thing, the first I freely willed to try. Together we'd done the hardest deed. . . . I also collected the awe they clearly showed at my strength, the first such admiration I'd had."[2]

I remembered yet again my priest friend Win's remark, "They have to kill the mother."

Price said that those days when his father died "were the fulcrum of my life, the point on which youth tilted into manhood. . . . I saw that the kindest thing Will Price did for me was to die when he did, when I stood on the doorsill of maturity. . . . [T]here in the generous absence of my father's huge presence, I began to move into that grown life I'd suddenly won. . . ."[3]

Win was speaking truthfully but metaphorically. He's had plenty of training in psychology and counseling, and he uses such language gently but directly in ministering to people like me. Reynolds Price, however, was speaking quite literally. He was twenty-one years and twenty-one days when his father died.

The time is coming soon, I thought. Cary is in college, and David is just four years behind her. Indisputably in the last half of my life, and with that life insurance payment declining quite precipitously these days, I could just about die now.

Well, I think on second thought I'll try to hang on just a *little* while longer. I'm not sure I have much appetite for presenting my

---

2. Reynolds Price, *Clear Pictures: First Loves, First Guides* (New York: Ballentine, 1988), 287–88, 295.

3. Ibid., 298–99.

own demise to my children for a twenty-first-birthday present and, now that I come to it, I am not very comfortable that Price considers his father's death a timely contribution to his own ascent to manhood.

I suspect there's life in me yet. Some new life that is setting buds, perhaps, and that will begin to flower in the years to come in ways that I cannot yet name. Maybe even in ways that will require less term life insurance.

In a Flowerpot

My friend Lee Ann asks me how Cary has been liking college this year. I tell her that Cary is so utterly certain that she is writing her own ticket that I think you could probably beat her about the head and shoulders with a blunt stick and she would still be happy. She insists on being the boss. She says that there are so many courses she wants to take that she hardly knows where to start.

It is too soon for her to know that we are less in control of the direction of life than we think. Perhaps it is important to have the joy of flight with your hands on the controls first.

I tell Lee Ann that I think Cary is like a pot of flowers you buy at the nursery that just can't wait to get out of the pot into the nice loose and welcoming soil of the prepared garden bed, to spread those pot-bound roots out and *really* get down to living.

I could have held Cary back from first grade another year because of her age, and I'd still have her at home this one more year, but I think it would have been a great mistake. She is all a-bloom.

Three A.M.

"Mom!" The imperative cry edged with panic came at three A.M. I was instantly awake the way I have responded to the sound of a child's cry for the past eighteen years.

There have been times when I would awaken and be in the hall so soon that my blood would still be rushing to my head, and I would have to stop for a second both to catch my balance and to listen for which room held the child in distress. But this time I had no doubt that it was Cary. I was out of bed, on my way to respond to her before good sense halted me. How silly. She isn't here. She's in Massachusetts. And no, David hadn't called me either. Anyway, his voice has changed, and this certainly was Cary's voice.

As I returned to bed my heart was still racing with that maternal surge born of both stark fear and the certainty that whatever is at hand—a child throwing up or having a bad dream—must and can be faced.

Cary was home for Thanksgiving these past few days. And yes, thank God, it was yet again the real Cary. Perhaps we had not exactly believed it would be. Yes, she had dyed her hair a lighter red, and yes, she intended to stay out past two each night with her friends and to skip church. But somehow the familiar person inside who is Cary was definitely there, and she went with us to cut a tree at a Christmas-tree farm. She and David ran and chased each other just as they had years ago, even wrestling and teasing and making up extravagant insults that degenerated into gales of laughter.

But Sunday afternoon she dismissed us from the airport before she boarded her plane. "I like hanging around in airports," she said. "I've traveled more than you have." She is right about that. We left her and plowed through the crowds of family members hugging one another good-bye, and went home.

Two hours later the phone rang. "I'm in the wrong airport! I got on the wrong plane!" Cary cried out, only very, very briefly being a child calling to her mother for rescue.

How, on the heaviest flying day of the flying year, could she have been seated in a reserved seat on a plane going to Washington National rather than BWI?

Have you gone to the airline for help, I asked? She had. She was on standby for the next flight to Hartford. And oh yes, she said, she had contacted the limo service at Bradley airport, to notify them of her later flight so that she could still get home to college.

Well, it seems that if I had been in charge, I would have done pretty much what she had already done. Good work, Cary, I said. She was warm, dry, safe, and booked onto the next flight. And she was quite calm now. An adult experiencing inconvenience and frustration, one of those momentary setbacks that life dishes up, but moving with the flow.

I noticed with pride, too, that she didn't place all the blame on the airline—after all, it is she who had boarded a plane when a flight other than hers had been called. (*I* was the one who was quite willing to blame the airline, but I'd certainly be mollified if they got her to Hartford tonight.)

Hours later I reached her by phone in her room. Oh yes, it all went off without a hitch, she said. No big deal.

I began breathing again. But I heard her call out to her mother in the middle of the night, and I leapt to her aid before I realized she was not there. As I tried to slow my heartbeat and lengthen my breaths to go back to sleep, I remembered that she had said on the phone, "I got home about eight-thirty—only an hour and a half late."

Indeed, her home is becoming elsewhere than here. And if it comes to me in the middle of the night in terror sometimes, at dawn my heart is proud and bright, and I know that it is very good indeed.

The Lame Walk and the Blind See

I am driving up Colley Avenue as I seem to do a dozen times a day, and I have just passed the Louise Eggleston Center sheltered workshop. Perhaps a dozen or so of the people who spend their days there—the mentally handicapped, the blind, the halt, and the lame—black and white, old and young, large and small, women and men, are out for a walk. They are holding one another's hands in a long serpentine line, moving very, very slowly past the playing fields of Blair Middle School, where ripe and able young children shout and run and play on the tennis courts, baseball diamond, and basketball court. Some of the walkers turn their heads to hear or see the children. I can almost physically sense from inside my car that they are intensely loving the fresh, crisp outside air, the beautiful day, and the children's clamor.

I consider the stark contrast between the line of disabled walkers and the vigorous, lovely young children for a minute and do the obvious—thank God for my abilities, for having two children of my own who do not suffer from any physical or mental disabilities. But this thought is eclipsed almost immediately as another awareness dawns on me.

This connected line of Eggleston folks wear their disabilities in very obvious ways. Their dependence on one another and on attendants who are charged with gently protecting them from harm is equally manifest. But perhaps we turn our heads away or recognize them as "other" precisely because they are more like us than we are willing to admit.

I am disabled and limited in a hundred ways, and so are my beautiful and competent children. I cannot make it through this perilous and confusing world without holding hands along the way. We guide each other as best we can, the blind sometimes indeed leading the blind, because the stumbling is inevitable, the path is treacherous, and going it alone is folly.

How long will it take to unmask the conceit and discover that rugged individualism and self-sufficiency are good policy only within very, very narrow circumstances? How foolish are we to conceal from our children that the very abilities and accomplishments we praise them for—their giftedness at the violin or in math, their soccer trophies and essay contest awards—will take them only so far and that along the way they are bound to need guidance and consolation too?

As I round the corner and head for home I find myself praying for this chain of people from the Eggleston center and for the people who look after them; for all whose dependencies are visible and for the middle-school children and all the rest of us who are walking so close to the edge and don't yet see our disabilities. I pray that we will all be tender and nurturing to one another, knowing that we're all in this boat together, needing one another, and needing God, to protect us and assure that we are guided in the right direction along the way, holding hands for dear life.

Pennies on the Railroad Track

"I'll be home on the train that gets into Newport News at eleven," Cary said over the telephone. "If you or Dad can't get me, see if Megan can." Megan is one of Cary's best friends from high school. She goes to college at Agnes Scott in Atlanta.

"That's okay," I said. "I can't be there, but I'm pretty sure your dad can get you."

"No, really," she said. "Megan likes to go to Newport News."

"Megan likes to go to *Newport News*?" You have to go through a usually impacted tunnel to get to this heavily industrial ship-building city.

"We used to go to the Amtrak station at night to put pennies on the railroad track and see what happened to them," she said. "Didn't I ever tell you?"

"*Cary*! You were hanging around a railroad yard at night?"

"Sure. It was fun. I don't do it anymore. See you at eleven." She rang off cheerfully.

Heaven only knows what she is doing *these* days. If I even learn about it years from now, I'll be lucky. Maybe I don't even want to know.

Christmas Vacation

My friend Ellen has been converting her daughter Katie's third-floor bedroom into a guest suite. Katie is a junior at William and Mary, and she has just left for Quito, where she will spend her spring semester.

Ellen is the one who urged me to buy Cary's plane tickets for Thanksgiving vacation in July, and she's a wise woman. Ellen also said that it was very important not to change a thing in Cary's room this first year, nothing except the sheets. By the junior year, she said, they are living in a lighter and lighter relationship with their rooms, their parents, their homes. Katie might spend the summer in Washington, after spending the whole semester in South America. She is considering the Peace Corps after graduation.

And that first Christmas vacation, Ellen said, is very important. I can see she is right. We moms have talked about this. The college freshmen are all behaving in the same way, and we don't like it much. We barely see them. They stay out very, very late at night— at the movies, at each other's houses, at the Open Door. Then they sleep until mid-afternoon. Cary barked at me yesterday noon when

I went into her room to give her the portable telephone. Not knowing whether I should feel hurt or scold her, I said nothing at all. Later she apologized. But honestly, feeling hurt and scolding seem rather beside the point just now.

One day this week, Cary managed to sleep until sunset. When she appeared downstairs, she announced, quite pleased with herself, "I think I have achieved nocturnalism!"

With little interest in dwelling on family relationships, or maybe with firm certainty that those relationships are static touchstones that can be taken for granted (for granite?), they spend all their time asleep or just "out," in each other's company. Nothing is interesting at home, which is supposed to stay the same. Friends, whose lives are rapidly changing, who are hitching rides on the four winds, now *they* are interesting. So, round everybody up and stay out at the Open House till all hours, have a go at catching up on all the news. Keep all those same pictures on the bedroom walls, but feel confident to step out into the maelstrom and see where it takes you. Maybe there can be all gain and no loss.

One by one, Cary's friends left and went back to school. She hadn't registered for a January-term class, but she asked to return to Massachusetts early. There was nothing much to do, and she wanted to go home, she said.

Birthday

We have talked on e-mail in ways that we would probably not talk face-to-face. We told some truths that we had not said before. About friends, and events long past. About fears and failings. About the perfectionism that is both blessing and curse.

She remembered my birthday with a card that quoted William Blake:

To see a world in a grain of sand
and a heaven in a wild flower,
hold infinity in the palm of your hand
and eternity in an hour . . .

Behind the verse on a very green background is the small figure of a woman, arms outstretched at her sides, facing into the surf and embracing the whole sea and the sky in an exuberant "Yes."

On the inside it says, "Happy birthday, Mom. I love you!"

Chapter 6—Another World

O God of peace, you have taught us that in returning
and rest we shall be saved,
in quietness and in confidence shall be our strength:
By the might of your Spirit lift us, we pray you,
to your presence,
where we may be still and know that you are God;
through Jesus Christ our Lord. Amen.[1]

Remembering

Journal entry, August 2, 1985. Cary is nearly six, David is two.

Geologists and biologists, I have heard, posit the existence of God for the sake of a Creator of the natural world. Mathematical types, perhaps, need an ultimate source of order and symmetry. Others require a confessor God; still others need a God of compassion. I've been a historian, and quite predictably, I guess, I feel the need for the existence of a God who notices and remembers everything. I couldn't bear it that there isn't somewhere in the universe a whole memory of the history of the world, down to the minutest detail. Call it a Recorder God and it sounds absurd, but still I have this hope and small faith that nothing of my children's childhood, their hopes and games and triumphs, my own growing into motherhood and through it, will be forgotten by God. This journal is only a small part of my need for sustaining memory, but I know what a tiny, insufficient job it does.

---

1. *The Book of Common Prayer*, 832.

Ann and Eleanor

My friend Ann lost her daughter when she was fourteen. Eleanor was inclined to bring her mom bouquets of fall leaves and to give her hugs for no apparent reason and say "I love you." She was also beginning to trumpet her adolescent independence and raise ferocious arguments. One day, on the way home from softball practice, she was killed by a car. Every fall when the leaves come down, Ann is visited by memories of Eleanor, and she marks her birthday. Eleanor would have been thirty this year. Ann might have had grandchildren by now.

I am sad beyond reckoning at this story. It is true that Ann never faced the voluntary letting go that would have come had Eleanor lived to draw her knife to cut the cord to her mother—to wield the cruel separating words, to turn away to her friends and wish her mother would leave sooner rather than later, to stop handmaking the birthday cards that professed eternal devotion. In unspeakable pain and mercy Eleanor remains locked in the moment of her death, never to suffer or inflict the suffering of the separation, never more to bring bouquets and surprises to delight her mother, never to come to herself into full flower and let Ann witness and endure the unfolding of her rich and mature individuality.

Love and loss lie so close to each other, so enfolded with each other, that the deftest surgeon could not part them, I suspect. I am incapable of comforting Ann and am doing a terrible job with myself. My guilt at still having a daughter alive prevents my revealing my loss adequately to Ann; her grief, renewed each fall and the deepest suffering of her life, will never depart from her. Yet our hearts have loved, in all the terrible pain of love, and we are sisters indeed; Cary and Eleanor who have never met, sisters too.

Nancy and Katie

Nancy has helped me this year more than she will ever know. Not only is she surrogate mom on call, but she's also taken my musings about letting Cary go seriously.

Nancy has just returned from a Christmas visit to Minnesota to see her daughter, a gifted musician, newly married and now expecting her first child. Katie plays and repairs flutes and plays the harp. Nancy writes:

I have loved all the stages my children went through, although I think I may have blanked out a lot of their teenage years. Even then, though, I looked at them with such wonder and admiration. I have just been to visit Katie. She gave me a tape of the combined choirs of three little Episcopal churches in the St. Paul area who got together and made a tape of the Rutter "Requiem." She plays harp on it, but I was not prepared for the impact it had on me. The tape was making its virgin voyage in my car tape player as I rounded one of the last turns to Hampshire this morning, and there, out of the midst of the sound, was the harp doing its harp thing. I thought, "That is really neat," and only then I realized it was my daughter. I broke down weeping. I was so overcome, as I have been many times, that my daughter, the oldest, the one I practiced on, has become such a full-blown adult, very different from me, but yet reflecting in a dim way both her father and me, and very much herself.

I guess this is by way of saying that I don't remember what my feelings were when the kids went off to college or to seek their fortune, how I felt to have one, then two, then three up and fly the nest; I probably buried sadness and loneliness in my work. But I love it now. It is certainly not worry-free, but it is definitely like holding the bird that flew in the window, warming it briefly, and then letting it fly away, trusting your temporary shelter and housing was just what it needed. It is very much an Easter feeling.

Nancy's son is an artist whose stained-glass pieces are throughout her house, and to see the sun come through all that dazzling rich color and intricate design is to know what a blessing it is to be allowed to raise children and let them go, for their colors and their music will always be with us, and the love in which we have wrapped them goes with them and then secretly returns to us.

Scarring

Cary's beautiful cherrywood-red hair is now, well, beautiful blonde. It was long and now it is short. There was one earring hole in each ear, and now there are two.

Many years ago my mother was patting me on the leg while we both watched television. "Oooh," she said when she touched my calloused foot. She was, in a certain way, wounded by the hard, abraded, damaged part of me.

"High mileage," I said. I have traveled far, and there's some scar tissue on me. I am quite certain that my mother looked at me in the cradle as I looked at Cary: as an unspoiled and perfect, pristine representative of all the possibility of humanity. That perfect baby body, that sweet wholeness. As a new mother, I believed I would do it all right. After all, I had read the books. I would protect her from the world. No, better still. I would make the world conform to her needs. Her nutrition would be excellent. Her teachers and schools would know her to be the precious jewel that she is and treat her accordingly. I would ward off all harm, remove all rocks in her path. More than that, I would teach her to recognize danger and repel it, to make good choices that honor herself, body and soul. I would not let evil scar her or the world pierce her with its rough, staining, indifferent cruelty.

My mother must have made these same resolutions. Yet just then she saw my feet, and she shook her head in dismay. What I first took merely as a criticism of me was not that at all. It was a *cri de coeur* of a mother like all mothers, who in a moment witnessed her own failure—not so much to produce a perfect child but to produce a perfect world to shield the child.

The children we launch into the world as innocents will be tossed and scarred. The world, of course, is cruel. But this is true as well: Many of the scars will be self-inflicted. The damage from an ill-advised climb into a tree whose branches were not sturdy enough to support the climber; the cold turned to pneumonia from staying up too late and continuing to smoke; the devastation of a broken relationship that was ill conceived from the beginning and ill tended along the way.

At the end of the day it seems to matter less than one might think whether we bear complicity in our own scarring. What seems more crucial is that it is inevitable and that no matter how we wish to shield our children, they will be tattooed with all that they endure, all that they flail their way past and through.

My mother caressed my poor feet, and now I pet Cary's blonde hair. I am thinking that all we need to know of grace is to accept and bless these outer manifestations of what marks and molds us in this life, for good or ill, however it all comes about. We offer these slightly battered but nonetheless courageously marching-ahead selves of ours to the future, asking God's mercy and blessing, maybe even God's caress.

Kids and Church

Michael, a man I talk to sometimes on the Internet, wrote that he'd begun going to church with his wife and two-year-old daughter. "I can't begin to tell you how positive the experience has been! I haven't been to church in twenty years. Looks like we have found a home. Wish I had done this some years ago."

I wrote back:

Dear Michael,

Thank God for kids, I guess. Your story is my story. Becoming a parent brought Bill and me back to church after dibbling around without commitment for years. We decided that going to church would be an every-Sunday event, no arguments or excuses or nego-tiations—rules applying to ourselves as well as to the children. And all has been made new, in a hundred ways. Going to church and loving it just kind of stuck. As a wise preacher said one day, "This is a wonderful place to fall in love with God."

But now our first child is exercising her natural right of defec-tion from the fold, and experimentation with apostasy. The second will surely soon do the same. College is the great divide.

I can't tell you how distressing this is to me, and I suspect I'm not just speaking for myself. I think there are plenty of parents who will tell the same story. At this point I have to realize that I cannot control this matter any longer for Cary. I cannot force-feed religion to her when she is six hundred miles away. My only options now are 1) to attend to my own faith, which, if you look at it with a funny squint, exists in a way because my children while in diapers evan-gelized me, 2) hope and pray that the message has gotten through to these beloved, if strong-willed, children, current appearances to the contrary notwithstanding, and 3) hand this problem over to God, to whom it has belonged, actually, all along, and who without doubt is quite competent to handle it.

I sounded a great deal more calm and confident than I really feel. But how much more can any of us do than plant the seed of what we believe and value with our children, and hope and trust for the best for them? If young adults in their late teens and twenties are poor church-attenders, we often blame the churches for doing "something wrong." Surely the services could be more lively and contemporary (or from what I see on church signs, the word must be "unplugged").

I think, though, that a time of feeling independent and self-sufficient, of flying high with grand aspirations that take little notice of frailty or contingency, suffering or compassion, is a natural thing. Youth reaches for transcendence and has little time for mortality. Time and life teach otherwise. One day they will reach out for the hand that, if they learned it in their childhood, they have known all along was there.

Certainly, God will continue to be loving Father and Mother to Cary even if she declines for the moment to meet her heavenly parent in church. In the same way, just as she must turn her back on Bill and me and our household to make her way in the world, while still trusting that she is always part of this family, she will range far afield from the grounding she has had in weekly church attendance.

I must come to my own place of trust and release. I hope my letting her loose is wise. I can hardly help it if it is not. In the final analysis, this is no longer my business to transact, and I am not an active player in the story of Cary's faith. The story will be written by the primary players themselves.

The Wall o' Rejections

"I've sent out over three dozen letters applying for internships," Cary writes in the spring. She wants to find some kind of work in the TV or movie industry, in New York or some other part of the country where she can find lodging with family or friends, and perhaps an office job on the side. "But the rejection letters are coming back. This is harder than I thought.

"However," she writes, "I have created a mammoth Wall o' Rejections in our hall, and everyone is posting all the letters that turn them down for anything. We're having a great time with it."

"Has anybody posted a letter from a boyfriend?" I ask by return post.

"Not yet," she answers cheerfully.

How *dare* anyone reject my daughter's application?

I entertained the possibility during that long year of college applications: Colleges might turn her down. I remember that all during her childhood, I would react extravagantly and unreasonably to the least criticism from her teachers, the smallest failure to recognize her talents. Attack *me* verbally, and you might get away with it, but attack my daughter? Think about nature films that you've seen of mother bears protecting their cubs and reconsider! All these years it's been hard for me to do what usually constitutes the best course of action: nothing. The urge to fix things has often been irresistible.

Last fall, around the beginning of November, Cary e-mailed us that she was dropping an art history class in mid-semester. It was too similar to the class she'd had her senior year in high school, and she didn't want to waste her time.

Surely, I said, you could complete this semester and earn the credit.

"Nope," she said. "To get credit for this semester, you have to take the next, and I'm bored looking at all the same pictures as last year. And don't suggest that I petition into a 200-level class next semester. I've already thought of that. The answer is no."

My urge was to call the dean.

"Please leave it alone and let me handle this," Cary said.

Are the academic advisers doing their job? I wondered. Couldn't I revert to her elementary-school days when I could go see the principal and straighten things out? How can the rules, regulations, and the very movement of the planets not be changed for my beloved?

How can anyone reject her application for an internship? And what can I do to comfort her in her disappointment?

Well, she appears to have devised quite a lovely response on her own, and it seems as though she's widened her ability to comfort herself to include all her friends. I wish I could sneak a peek at that Wall o' Rejections and maybe even catch a glimpse of young women gratefully turning their failures into defiant merriment.

The Mother's Face

"You learn the world from your mother's face. You learn about God from the way she moves, how she loves or doesn't love, how she smells, what she says in words and silence. You learn about creation from the way your parents love each other, the story they tell you about how they came together to make you. These details

create your idea of who you are and where you came from, the color, texture, depth, or shallowness of your universe, the particular tangle of roots that brought you out of the ground."[2]

There's more than a little irony in this statement Mark Matousek makes, because his mother was pretty much the epitome of dysfunction, and his life was a hard one. When he wrote this book, he was dying of AIDS, and only near the end did he find a surrogate mother who could love him unconditionally and who could lead him deep within himself to discover divine love as well, in preparation for death.

But this also leads me to consider that what flows from mother to child can never be wholly perceived by the child, and what the child sees in the mother's face can never be wholly understood by the mother.

Children cannot know the full depth or the unrelenting passion with which they are loved, from the moment of intoxication with the sweetness of the smell of a baby's head or the delight of those little toes and ears, to the agony of watching the child in despair over a lost game or a bad grade or a cutting remark. If children knew the dimension of this love, they might never be able to bear it, might have to avert their gaze from its intensity.

I think a parent who insists that this overwhelming love be returned reciprocally probably damages some great design. Better that the love be received and then transformed and passed down the

---

2. Mark Matousek, *Sex Death Enlightenment: A True Story*
(New York: Riverhead Books, 1996), 28.

line. Better to imagine with joy the time when Cary will become a mother, for instance, and delight in her own baby, believing that the overfilling of her heart is so new and unique that the whole universe seems to have been created anew.

We parents can never fully know what our children think of us. I am sure our hearts would be broken to know the extent to which our children believe we have hurt them, when we love them so deeply and desperately. We parents joke about what our children will tell their therapists about us in years to come, but behind the joke is a real fear that the parenting we intended to be flawless has not measured up. And it's not so much the thought of being blamed that saddens our hearts but the thought that what was meant as love became corrupted and caused suffering.

On the other hand, we might be equally shocked to learn how very little they think of us at all. Perhaps these are things it is best not to know. We may need to look in a different direction altogether. At a photograph I have, for example, of Cary when she was nearly four. She is wearing a green gingham sundress that I made for her, and she is sitting on a hospital bed with her newborn brother. It is the first time she has seen him. She is holding a toy, a gift she chose, in the air above David's head, shaking it so that the camera sees only a multicolored blur. Her gaze is focused intently on the baby, and the baby's on her. In the entire history of art, I know of no sweeter or purer Madonna's face. I cherish this picture more than I can say.

I believe I will insist on hoping this for myself and for all of us: that by the grace of God our faces and our stories, and the ways we have treated our children from the time we nursed them and changed their diapers, are imprinted on them as an abiding love that, as they grow strong and healthy and good, they will barely notice or call by name, but whose seed they will nurture until it comes to flower in their lives and their relationships—in their art, in their care for themselves, in their worship, and above all in their own children. As God himself must know, love flows down and out more perfectly than back to its source, in a way that multiplies its effect in the world and brings all into the possibility of full bloom.

Atoms

Cary isn't sure she wants to come home for spring vacation. She wants phone conversations to be short. She has plans.

I do my work in the dining room, which doubles as an office; David inhabits the den and plays his guitar along with Dave Matthews recordings; Bill tries to find a place to work—a nomad with a laptop.

We all test "introvert" on the Myers-Briggs indicator test. We seem like atoms that repel each other rather than an organism that works together.

David says, in a moment of angry eloquence, hurling an insult over some offense he perceives, "We have nothing in common except that we live under the same roof and have the same last name!" And he goes to the telephone to find friends who will help him with whatever is bothering him.

In our culture I think we have bought into a utopian vision of the ideal family, eating dinner and playing Scrabble together, sharing their every thought and emotion, laughing and traveling and problem solving in a well-oiled, interdependent unit where selfishness and the desire to be alone never intrude. I measure our family of four against the model of the 1950s sitcom, and we fall very, very short. There's so much free-floating blame for the failure of the family these days that I could feel guilty all the time. I have a creeping suspicion that we all fall short in this way or that, yet it's terribly hard to admit it to each other. Have *you* done this better than we have? Are there dinners together every night, soccer and homework phone calls be damned? Do all the family members bare their souls to each other, and are decisions made by consensus? Is authority always recognized, and always wise, and do the children obey their parents, knowing that fair and consistent penalties will always be the consequence otherwise? Are there kisses before leaving the house every morning, and fond hugs in the evening? Does the family spend Saturday evenings with each other, playing Monopoly with the television off? Would each person name a family member as his or her "best friend"?

Is the family supposed to cohere, or is it natural for its parts to fly off at a tangent? When my children *do* fly off on a tangent of their own devising, must I be burdened with guilt?

What is the family for, and what is a child supposed to learn by living in a family? Do we really share only a last name and then zoom off in our own directions? Should I feel guilty to have children forge their way into the world outside without being tied to backward glances, wishing instead that they remain dependent on the sense that sweetness and security can be found only at home? Are families made up of introverts a matter for shame? Has the glue that holds our family together been so watery, our cohesion so faint, that we all just drift off as single atoms in a dark universe where our chances to bond with each other get more remote all the time? Or might I hope that launching these children into the world without requiring them to be yanked back by ties of dependency or guilt is success enough?

Dream

The house is cluttered and dimly lighted, filled with people, overfilled with furniture and unlabeled boxes lining the walls and stacked on top of each other. Every room would take an hour to describe: There is so much in it, and so much has happened in it. There is noise and activity everywhere, and dust, and it is barely possible to move from one room to the next through corridors and hallways partially blocked with piles of newspapers and old clothes.

But I find a door I've never seen before, and I walk through it to find a suite of rooms: a sitting room, a bedroom, and a bathroom. The walls are all painted pale, pale yellow with gleaming white woodwork, and the windows are open. A gentle breeze lifts the sheer white curtains, and the fresh air gently moves through open,

clean, and uncomplicated space, in silence. It is very light in the
rooms, but not glaringly so. I am drawn in, careful to close the door
behind me, because I know that this is my place and mine alone, a
place of delight and infinite possibility, of promise and blessing and
new life. I can visit it anytime I want, anytime at all.

Lamaze Exercises

When Cary was born, the Lamaze method for coaching during natural childbirth was not wholly new, but new enough that we had to deliberately shop for an obstetrician and a hospital friendly to it. I remember attending the classes that prepared Bill and me for labor and delivery, and the huffing and puffing exercises that used regular, repeated breathing patterns to induce, it seemed to me, a kind of self-hypnosis during contractions. I sometimes still use these techniques to good advantage in the dentist's chair. Dr. Marshall asks me (alarmed to notice a bit of hyperventilation going on) if I am all right. I grunt that I am fine. I figure: He's got two children. He should know what I'm doing.

I also remember that during the Lamaze classes all those years ago, we would take turns lying on floor exercise mats, trying to follow the cheerful teacher's instructions on how to relax. She would begin with one body part and go on to the next. Your foot is completely relaxed, she would say, it is infinitely heavy and you cannot move it. There are no muscles or nerves; your foot is sinking into the mat. And, moving on to the calf and the knee, she would convince us that no matter what the stimulus, we would relax completely. It was all a matter of concentration. I would listen and try to make myself into no more than an inert sack of flour, lying on a rubber mat. I was a shade skeptical about this, but I faithfully practiced relaxing, and I took some small comfort that there were other pregnant women in the same boat with me.

The principle behind these Lamaze techniques, I presume, is that when the uterus is contracting, the rest of the body should relax to help it out—that is, if your body can "go with the flow" of childbirth, those babies will somehow pop out more successfully. I think I applied these lessons far from perfectly when I gave birth to Cary and David, but they were born healthy, and I was awake for the show.

The Lamaze exercises seem to offer an apt lesson for these latter days of mothering. There is another giving-birth going on, another process of labor and delivery, and to fight it by fussing and straining, pulling in ways that cross the grain of what is inevitable and timed by the child will cause distress for everybody concerned.

Is it inevitable that there is pushing and pain? I suppose so. But somehow I believe that I have a choice of aligning myself with it or against it, of relaxing into it or not. I think those Lamaze instructors were right. Moreover, having the company of that coach, who's seen it before and can lead you along—the good husband, the good friend, the calm companion—is worth all the huffing and puffing in the world.

Elijah and the widow of Zarephath

In time of drought, the prophet Elijah is on the road. God has promised that he won't starve or parch, but things are tough everywhere he goes. Arriving in the town of Zarephath, he obeys God's command to ask for food from a certain widow.

He finds the woman out gathering firewood. Bring me water please, he says. And while you're at it, bread.

I swear I have nothing but a little flour and a little oil, she says. I'm on my way home to make a tiny bit of bread for my son and me, and after that we shall starve. How can I feed you?

Don't worry, says Elijah. Do as I say and you will have enough flour and oil for many days to come, until it rains again.

So, she goes home and does as Elijah said, and bakes bread for him, and the flour bowl and the oil jar refill themselves. Elijah moves in as a lodger.

A while later, the woman's son gets sick and dies. She appeals to Elijah, blaming him a bit, if truth be known—saying, if you had not come to live with me, my son would be well.

Elijah takes pity on her. He receives the lifeless boy from his mother and carries him upstairs to his own room, and he prays, asking God why he would bring calamity on this poor widow.

Then he stretched himself upon the child three times, and cried out to the Lord, "O Lord my God, let this child's life come into him again." The Lord listened to the voice of Elijah; the life of the child came into him again, and he revived. Elijah took the child, brought him down from the upper chamber into the house, and gave him to his mother: Then Elijah said, "See, your son is alive." So the woman said to Elijah, "Now I know that you are a man of God, and that the word of the Lord in your mouth is truth."[3]

We spend what we have, and more is returned to us. We entrust our beloved children to what we hope is the care of God, of a benevolent world, of a just outcome where hard work and virtue will bring happiness and all good things. But before we know that abundance will come back to us and our children will be awakened to new life, we have to make an appalling leap of faith, to spend and let go. So very hard to do when you can't quite be sure that it's Elijah out there asking.

Models and Turning Fifty

It's the oddest birthday artwork I've ever received, and like all mothers, I have a unique collection that I wouldn't part with for the world. This is a rough wooden plank, painted gold, inscribed with a message. To the left and the right of the message are beautiful models in swimsuits, magazine cut-outs découpaged onto the board, but some of them taller than the board itself. All the women are slim, fit, and cool, and many have their arms languidly lifted over their heads as they stare off into the distance. Upon closer inspection it seems that all the beauties on the left margin are looking toward the center of the wooden plank, and the handful on the

---

3. I Kings 17:19–24 (*New Revised Standard Version*).

right are looking inward as well, as if they are coolly regarding the handwritten words.

The birthday message reads:

Ever wonder why models are always
Gazing wistfully off into the distance?
Because they're jealous of you and your life!
That's right—A life in which a girl can
Do her job without having to have her nipples
Airbrushed out—A life in which she is not
Judged by her various bodily circumferences
But by what she can do, and most
Importantly—A life in which
She's allowed to age, however gracefully,
Past 35. So feel lucky to be 50, and
Be glad, as are we all, that this is
1997 instead of 1697—when the life
Expectancy was like 30, except for
Models, who were publicly
Executed before the age of 20.
Happy Birthday.
Love, Cary

Wanting and Doing

"I can't believe I got what I wanted," Cary said, in that spring of her last year in high school. She was referring to scholarship offers that allowed her to choose among some private colleges that she knew we couldn't afford otherwise. Maybe there was the smallest admixture of guilt in there with her delight and triumph, that she could have what many people couldn't.

"Well," I said, "you earned it. You did it yourself."

Not many of her public-school classmates would be going out-of-state for college. Only a handful apparently wanted to, for one thing, and Virginia has a number of good colleges. But those who wished to leave Virginia would have to find scholarship money for private colleges, pay out-of-state tuition for public colleges, or have parents who could manage a tuition bill in the tens of thousands.

"Look forward to it," I said. "You'll be among smart kids who actually read *Hamlet* when it was assigned and liked it. Kids who draw and sculpt and understand puns."

Cary has never been shy about saying what she wants and standing her ground. In the second grade, she dug in her heels, refused to continue piano lessons, and won the day. I worry sometimes, mostly when I'm awake at three A.M., that I'm a terrible mother because I allowed my children to make so many decisions themselves, especially about their out-of-school activities, their haircuts, and their wardrobes. Their choices often wouldn't have been mine. But as some of my sympathetic friends have said, you pick your battles. All her life, well-behaved kid that she has been, Cary has carefully honed the ability to decide what she wants and then proceed to get it.

Late in her junior year of high school, she wondered out loud whether it was really necessary to take calculus as a senior, or whether instead she could break out of the mold of the expected curriculum and take Art History. I had to admit that given her interests, art seemed like a great idea to me. But I was inclined to think that the colleges would expect math.

So, together we called the admissions offices at her top four college choices, and we talked with the admissions officers on duty. To my amazement, all four said exactly the same thing. If you love art and not math, take art. We like to see students who know their own minds and who stretch to do unique things, especially difficult ones.

Cary would be taking five AP classes that senior year, but she said, "I'm going to enjoy the whole year because of this."

I wish I could tell Smith College that never have they had a student enter their portals so determined that she had gotten what she wanted when they admitted her, so certain that she would be happy in her next four years.

I'm proud of her determination. Just as a new mother is pleased to learn that her baby knows how to comfort itself with a thumb or a blanket, the mother of a child leaving home takes comfort herself in knowing that her eighteen-year-old can name what she wants and go get it.

But, I reflect, it is nòt quite this simple. I must be honest. The older I am, the more I must confess that I don't control as much in life as I'd like to claim. Seldom is the line between "I want" and "I have" very straight. It is not only that misfortune and grief befall us all unbidden; it's that so much seems to be accidental or an unforeseen consequence. Often events appear to be caused by the decisions that were not the momentous ones but the little ones that demanded so little thought or regard.

I have raised my beloved children as all of us diligent parents have: We have told them to work hard, learn self-discipline, choose wisely, and anticipate consequences. I can't imagine doing otherwise. And yet . . . and yet. Do hard work and discipline always bring results? Can you avoid being treated badly by people you cannot control, or in circumstances that are random or malign? Can any of us realistically believe that we will not have to depend on other people, or that some of the people we depend on may be careless or incompetent or wicked?

Can we really ever get everything we want? Can we even choose what we want with sufficient wisdom to guarantee an end product worth having?

Both of my children asked me, when they were very little, whether they would die.

"Yes," I said, "but not until you are very old."

"Am I old?" Cary asked.

"No, you are very young. It will be a long, long time before you die."

"Are you old enough to die?"

"No," I answered, "I will not die for a very long time, either."

But I knew as I gave these answers that I was dealing in statistical probabilities and answering more with an intent to comfort than to tell the truth. I was promising what isn't in my power to promise.

When Cary was about fourteen, a school friend of hers died of a broken neck in a car accident. The foundations of Cary's world came unhinged. Dozens of young people attended Angela's funeral, which was held in a huge, bleak, cinder block–walled naval base chapel. I have never witnessed such despair and forlorn lostness as this. There was a contingent of NROTC students in uniform: boys and girls dressed as if adult naval officers. There were girls in dresses and boys in shirts and ties that they wouldn't be caught dead in otherwise, trying to deal with a grief that was utterly beyond them. Beyond me.

Wouldn't be caught dead in.

I suppose that with all our children, somehow all will be well, in ways that are wholly beyond my comprehension, and that venture into the realm of faith. I know that I have to raise children to work hard and make good choices. I know that I must give them a sense that they have power to do good in this world. But day by day I grow more certain that the power to effect outcomes is only partly in my grasp. I am left to trust in the grace of God that all will be well, in ways God understands far better than I do.

It Won't Be Long Now

I just had a premonition so vivid I could almost taste and smell it.

One day not long from now this household's phone will ring fewer than five times a day. There will be a month in which no pizza is delivered to our front door. Objects placed on a surface will be in the same place five days later. Doing laundry will be an occasional event. Budgeting will be possible, and there will be no surprise purchases involving sporting equipment or rock concerts. There will be no arguments for the sake of argument alone, and there will be no underwear, socks, or towels lying on the floor of the downstairs bathroom. The bolt on the back door can be secured at bedtime, and I will not sleep with one ear open for a returning teenager.

And Bill and I will have the luxury of rediscovering what it was we saw in each other when we decided to spend the rest of our lives together about three decades ago.

Blessing

With pen and ink and paints, I once wrote out this poem by Edward Carpenter for Cary. But now I see. It must have been at least half for me from the very beginning. It is called "The Lake of Beauty."

Let your mind be quiet, realising the beauty of the world,
* and the immense, the boundless treasures that it holds in store.*
All that you have within you, all that your heart desires,
* all that your Nature so specially fits you for—that or the*
* counterpart of it waits embedded in the great Whole, for you.*
* It will surely come to you.*

Yet equally surely not one moment before its appointed time
* will it come. All your crying and fever and reaching out of*
* hands will make no difference.*

Therefore do not begin that game at all.
Do not recklessly spill the waters of your mind
    in this direction and in that,
    lest you become like a spring lost
    and dissipated in the desert.

But draw them together into a little compass, and hold them
    still, so still;
And let them become clear, so clear—so limpid, so mirror-like;
at last the mountains and the sky shall glass themselves in
    peaceful beauty,
and the antelope shall descend to drink and to gaze at her
    reflected image, and the lion to quench his thirst,
and Love himself shall come and bend over and catch his
    own likeness in you.[4]

Joining the Circus

"I just don't know what to do about my granddaughter," a friend at church confides in me, her face lined with worry and woe. She knows Cary is in college now, so she expects a sympathetic ear. She also knows full well that one can't do much about granddaughters.

"She joined the circus."

This sounds like a story from a different era. Or from a fairy tale.

---

4. Quoted in *A New Zealand Prayer Book*, 157.

"Colleen has wanted to be a trapeze artist ever since she was little and first went to the circus. Her mother thought it was a passing fancy, but she took her to gymnastics classes and so on. Colleen was very good at gymnastics, and very daring, but still. Who imagines that their daughter will actually join the circus?"

I was fascinated, and my friend could see it. She went on.

"Her mother and father—my daughter and her husband, you know—told her that they would permit her to join the circus, but only if she would graduate from college first, from a good college. Colleen agreed. She went to Wellesley, and she graduated in four years with a double major in international relations and economics.

"But her mother and father were wrong in thinking that it was a passing fancy, because then Colleen more or less demanded that her parents keep their part of the bargain, since she'd kept her part. And they have. She is on tour with Ringling Brothers. Every day I pray that she will not fall and be paralyzed or killed. I have seen a videotape of her, practicing her routine or her performance or whatever you call it, and she is very good. She is quite beautiful up there in the air, actually. But she could so easily break her neck."

What will Cary claim as her freedom not so long from now? How will she risk her neck in ways that I find foolhardy? I suppose I hope to have the wisdom of Colleen's parents to say yes and let her go. I hope I will follow in my friend's footsteps and watch the videotape, all the while saying my prayers. I also hope I'll follow her lead in seeking the solace of friends, for we are all in this together. None of our daughters belongs to us, but in a way, they are all ours. And as we watch them soar high above our heads, letting go of the bar and flying through the air, no hands, we hope that one day we can stop holding our breath and just marvel at their exquisite beauty and freedom.

Another World

Journal entry, March 30, 1985. Cary is six, David two.

I was walking early today along a side street in Richmond, Virginia, past the walled-in garden of a very old house. As I strolled along the brick path, I smelled warm, wet, flowery spring smells, and I had a brief whiff of another, alternative existence, whether of a self that used to be, or one that might be. Perhaps it came to me because I was a hundred miles away from family and home—a rare event indeed. I have been visited before with these whiffs—evocative and fleeting and somehow very primitive.

What these experiences tell me is that my life, while incredibly full, intense, and satisfying, is narrowly circumscribed, as if one thoroughly investigated a mine shaft but never saw the landscape or the sun, as if one devoted a life to black-and-white photography but never tried painting or sculpture or colors. The infinite possibility of life beckons me with these whiffs, but there seems to be no exit, at least right now, from my circumscription, from the walls of my garden. I don't know exactly where I am being called to, but I have these tiny glimpses under the veil.

Motherhood unquestionably adds to my life a thousand times more than it subtracts. Now that Cary and David exist there is a new universe, and I am bound to them by ties that are stronger than life and death. I have been altered forever, and I am devoted to this new life.

Yet I can't help but be attracted to these other worlds. Once Cary and David get older, will that other world still beckon me with its scent, and will the doors still be unlocked? Will I have to leave Cary and David behind? I'm not sure whether I could ever endure a world not utterly filled with them.

There are women (and men too of course) who in their middle years leave their families, change careers, have affairs, or (short on grand courage) get frizzy permanents or radically change their appearance. Perhaps they are walking in Bill's and my shoes. Perhaps my smells of spring in a Richmond garden are just a preview for me. I don't want to leave anything behind, certainly not Bill. I don't want frizzy hair. But that earthy smell of possibility and promise is worth tucking into a very safe place and holding onto.

The Flower in the Crevasse

I have Cary's charcoal sketch framed above my desk and computer. She doesn't know why of all her artwork, I like this best. But the more I have to accommodate myself to her absence from this house, the more I love and am frightened by this picture.

The whole paper is filled with mountainous terrain, but framed in the lower center by all the cragginess is a single flower, bold and upright and standing alone, way down in a crevasse. High on the right is the figure of a young woman, certainly Cary herself, it seems to me. Her whole body bends in desire toward the flower as she stands on a ledge, her hair swinging forward to obscure most of her face. Her arms reach together almost in supplication toward it, hands parted, stretching as far as possible and risking falling down the cliff. Her whole being yearns downward toward the flower. The focal point of the picture almost seems to be the charged empty space in between girl and flower.

But higher still on the right, anchored to a kind of reality represented by the edge of the paper into which it fades, is another figure, neither clearly male nor clearly female. This person cannot reach Cary but stands with a look of alarm and protective worry on his or her face, arm stretched out as if to try to catch her from falling, eyebrows raised in fright, mouth round and open in warning. This is a guardian, a caring and open-faced loving person, but someone calling halt. Cary is ignoring all the warnings and all the imploring. She will do what she will do, and there is no question that the flower beckons her. If I were to find myself or Bill in the picture, it would obviously be that guardian that Cary has shaken herself loose from.

The picture worries me when I look at it, for the danger of her falling makes me catch my breath every time, and the mountains are very steep and treacherous. I am unquestionably the worrier in the picture, the cautious one who cannot fathom just why this flower is so all-fired important. But I stand back from the picture and marvel at the beautiful yearning, the reaching for freedom, the intent focus on the prize. I believe once more, with solemn gratitude and joyful heart, that the daughter of my own flesh is good, and strong, and free, and that no matter what the odds or how tough the terrain, she will not be deflected from her quest for beauty and wonder in this life, God bless her.